Dare to Be Different

BY *Fred Hartley:*

UPDATE
DARE TO BE DIFFERENT

Dare to Be Different
Dealing with peer pressure

Fred Hartley

ILLUSTRATIONS BY GENE HAULENBEEK

Fleming H. Revell Company
Old Tappan, New Jersey

Library of Congress Cataloging in Publication Data

Hartley, Fred.
    Dare to be different.

    1. Youth—Conduct of life.   2. Social
pressure.ˑ I. Title.
HQ796.H353   305.2ʹ3   80-93
ISBN 0-8007-5041-1

TO
my two children,
Fred Allan IV and Andrea Joy,
for whom I hope to set an example
as I *dare to be different*

Contents

1
The Silent Influence

"PEER PRESSURE" are two words no one likes to use. Parents hate the expression because it describes to them the way their sons or daughters are going to the dogs. Young people hate the words because in a do-your-own-thing generation, to copy someone else's behavior is the unforgivable sin. Therefore, these words are usually avoided, even though peer pressure is in most of our subconscious minds and is a silent influence upon most of our lives.

When I was in high school, I would come home after football practice and sit down at the dinner table. My dad would ask me, "Hey, what did you do at school today, Fred?" Usually, I would just grunt. Well, he did not like grunts; so he would say something like, "Come on! You must have done something today, and your mother and I would like to hear about it." With no possible escape, I would proceed to tell them a few details.

It seemed that, without fail, we would drift into a tense discussion over legalizing marijuana, the Vietnam War, racism, or how late I should stay out on weekends. Things would usually cool down over dessert; but, often, when I would leave the table, I could overhear one of them saying, "I just don't like the way Fred is being influenced at school."

Have you ever heard your parents talk about the way your friends are influencing your life? If you are the way I was, your response is to insist that you are *not* being influenced by them, and you reject what your parents say. For some reason, we don't like to admit that we are actually afraid of what other people think and that we actually copy their behavior.

Types of Peer Fear

We cannot put every way that the crowd influences us into the same sink and then flick on the garbage disposal. We must admit there are many different ways in which our friends can influence us, and they are not all bad. Basically we can divide up the influences into three categories:

(1)   Good influences
(2)   Neutral (plain vanilla) influences
(3)   Bad influences

1. Good Influences   It is a basic human need to be accepted and loved. You show me someone who doesn't desire either of these, and I'll show you a toad. We all need to be held and kissed and laughed with. We were not created to function like frantic little electrons, constantly circling past each other without ever coming in contact with anyone. We were made to live in community and to have friends. And we need friends. We need people to say, "Hey, you are okay. I like to be with you."

Stanley never had many friends. He wasn't involved with any sports or clubs at school. All he had was a rabbit. Every day he'd get out of school, go straight home, grab some carrots, and go feed his rabbit. All afternoon he'd watch his rabbit munch on carrots. One day I went over to Stanley's house, and we got out the soccer ball, dusted it off (because he never played with it), and started kicking it around. Stanley surprised himself: He could actually kick a soccer ball.

That year he went out for the soccer team and made it. Pretty soon that ingrown guy who never did much, other than stare at his carrot eater, began to blossom as a person. He came out of himself and began making friends.

After one of the soccer games, Stanley's mother came up to me and whispered in my ear, "Thank you so much for taking an interest in Stanley. He was always such a loner, but now he is really happy and full of life."

At the time I really didn't know why she said that to me, because I was unaware of doing anything for Stanley. But, as I look back, that one afternoon when I got sick of looking at Stanley's rabbit and suggested that we play soccer must have influenced Stanley to get more involved in life. Stanley's mom obviously didn't mind that type of peer influence on her son. In fact, she was quite excited about it. There are many ways in which our friends can have good influences upon our lives.

2. *Neutral (Plain Vanilla) Influences* The crowd can influence us in ways that can be categorized as neither good nor bad. For the most part, clothing styles are neither good nor bad; and virtually all of us are influenced by what our friends wear. Girls' hairstyles are greatly influenced by how the rest of the members of the gang are getting their hair cut, and there is nothing ethically good or evil about a particular hairstyle. What sport to go out for in a particular season, what club to join, what classes to take, what party to go to on weekends, and so on, are all partially determined by what our friends decide to do. None of these are particularly good or bad.

Let me give you a strange example of a neutral influence. My parents always taught me good table manners, and they insisted on them. When I went to high school, I can still remember the first week of eating in the cafeteria, with all the new faces I was trying to get to know. Before long I noticed a lot of soup slurping and lip smacking—things forbidden around our home. Well, it didn't take someone long to make the comment, "Who's your mother—Emily Post? Good grief, I've never seen such etiquette!" So, to avoid the conflict, I started slurping my soup and making a little more noise when I ate.

A few weeks later, I sat down with my parents at the dinner table, and my mother served soup. "Slurp! Slurp! Slurp!" I wasn't aware of it, but I was drinking soup the way we drank it at school.

"Fred!" my mother cried, "who taught you to eat soup like that?"

I didn't have the heart to tell her. "Oh, sorry, Mom."

Thus, I learned to eat soup two different ways, depending on whom I was with.

Ultimately, it is no big deal how we eat our soup, as long as the people we are with don't get sick to their stomachs. There are a lot of neither good nor bad ways in which we are influenced by our friends. They are just okay plain vanilla.

3. Negative Influences Although our friends can have good influences upon us, we must admit they can also have negative influences upon us. This is the area in which peer pressure gets a bad name.

It was strange to be one of the few kids in sixth grade who did not swear. It was also strange to be one of the few virgins in the senior class of high school. The pressure to swear got to me, and I began to use a whole new vocabulary. The pressure to have sexual intercourse did not get to me, and I am glad that it didn't. There was one night, however, when I had to defend my moral standard.

I was watching horror movies at Howard's house, as I often did on Saturday nights, when, during one of the commercials, Howard went over to check the door, to make sure his parents weren't around. Then he got a strange smirk on his face and said, "I went to bed with a girl the other night."

I was munching on popcorn, so I pretended I had choked on a kernel. This was a topic I was not used to talking about, and I didn't know what to say, so I said nothing. I just watched the commercial and ate popcorn.

After a few moments, Howard mocked, "What's wrong with you? Haven't you ever taken a girl to bed before? Everybody is doing it."

As long as he was pressing me on it, I figured there was no choice but to respond. "No, Howard, I don't intend to take a girl to bed until she is my wife, and then I am sure it will be fantastic!"

At that point I think he called me a few names like Prude or Straight or Holy Joe. At the time it didn't bother me, because Howard was the first of all my friends to go off and have premarital sex. He seemed, at the time, to be the oddball. But, later, after several more of my close friends started, I was in the minority. The tide changed and started to move against me, and I was often tempted to give in to the way "everybody else" was living. I am glad I never did.

I spent almost two years living on an island in Florida, and it was the "cool" thing to get the youngest kids possible to be trained in shoplifting. The younger the kid, the greater the crowd approval. They called it the five-finger discount. Believe it or not, some first and second graders became so skilled that they could walk off with just about anything they wanted, and the store owners would not suspect a thing.

We could look at an endless list of negatives: swearing, drunkenness, loose sex, cheating on tests, disobedience to parents, lying, smoking marijuana, boasting, mocking, shoplifting, and so on. Basically they all come under the same category: They are all moral issues. These activities are more than simply slurping soup. They are moral issues because it is possible to distinguish a right and a wrong choice. Therefore our friends can have a hazardous effect upon us when they tempt us to compromise our moral standards.

Have you ever done something you knew was wrong, just to gain the approval of friends? If you have a moral standard on any issue, have you ever found it hard to stand alone? If you don't have any moral standards now, try to remember back to when you did. Whether it be smoking grass or having sex, can you remember how awkward you felt when all your friends were already involved and you were not?

Right now, be honest with yourself. You have no reason to impress me. And you have no reason to defend yourself. Just be honest and think about what are (or have been) some of the moral standards you have had difficulty holding to while the rest of your friends have forgotten them.

Feelings

1. Do your parents ever accuse you of being affected by peer pressure? How does it make you feel?
2. Do you like to talk with your parents? Why or why not?
3. Have your parents ever embarrassed you? When?
4. Tell about the first time you felt pressured to lower a moral standard.
5. Describe what it would be like to have no friends.
6. Can you remember the first time you ever felt guilty?

Thoughts

1. Who is a better listener: you or your parents?
2. What do your parents nag you about?
3. Why do kids like to be unique?
4. What are some good influences your friends have had in your life?
5. What are moral standards?
6. How do we decide what moral standards are worth keeping?
7. Why do we feel guilty sometimes?
8. Are there any negative ways in which your friends have influenced your life?

2
Please, Don't Mock Me Out

THE MOST IMPORTANT thing in the life of a teenager is usually his own name. After all, adolescence is the time when we start finding out all about ourselves. We start spending more and more time in front of the mirror, asking questions like, "Am I cute? Does my hair look right? Am I sexy? Can I dance?"

In the late sixties, the rock group known as the Who produced a rock opera called *Tommy*. The plot centered around a boy, Tommy, who wasn't known for anything special. He didn't have a reputation for anything—until he turned on to pinball. The feature song in the opera is "Pinball Wizard," which pictures all Tommy's friends standing around him, cheering him on as the greatest of all pinball players. Tommy gained a reputation that meant more to him than anything in life.

Similarly, John Travolta, starring in the hit movie "Saturday Night Fever," played the part of a "nobody" who got interested in disco dancing and became the best of all disco dancers. He went from being a nobody to being *somebody*. He gained a reputation that meant more to him than anything in life.

We all have a deep inner need to be loved, to be held and kissed, to be laughed with, and to be accepted. These things are as important to us as oxygen and water. We can't live without them. Some of us bounce from group to group, trying to find a place to belong and a friend who will stand beside us, no matter what we do. For most of us, there is no greater desire within us than to have a best friend. This acceptance is worth more, to many of us, than food or sleep. For others, who already have a friend, a reputation might be the highest treasure. Some people so lust for a name that they are willing to do anything to "be cool."

Ouch! I Felt That Mock

You show me someone who says he's never been hurt by a mock, and I'll show you a liar. It is tough to be a kid in a cut-down society, especially when teenagers are the sharpest critics. It is hard to think of a day at school in which someone does not get mocked out. And yet, the crazy thing is that we all hate it when we are the ones who get mocked. In fact, there is nothing we hate more. Nothing hurts more, so we usually live in fear of it—fear of peers. The nub of peer fear is the mock.

Some of us live in constant fear of being mocked out. The boy with the scrawny body fears taking his shirt off in the locker room, because of what his friends might say. The girl with the new haircut fears walking on campus, because of the jokes that her friends might make.

I can remember the first day of Physical Education, when we all went into the locker room, changed into our gym clothes, and walked into the weight room. We all lined up alphabetically, to be tested at different skills. I was fairly athletic and not very concerned. The first test was chin-ups, and the first kid couldn't do any. "Ha, ha, ha!" Man, did we ever let him have it. "You toothpick! You probably couldn't even pull yourself out of bed in the morning." That boy felt like crawling under the floor boards.

As the next few kids were doing their chin-ups, the thought passed through my mind, *What if I can't do any, either?* I panicked! *Oh, no! What will I do?* Soon it was my turn. I froze. They called my name twice, and I acted as if I didn't hear. Then, finally, I walked over, jumped up, and grabbed the bar. I felt as if I were dangling over a pit of hungry lions. *What if I can't do a chin-up?* Grunt. Grunt. Grunt. *Ahhhhhh!* I was safe! I had done three chin-ups. I made it. Nobody laughed at me. Nobody mocked me, and I breathed a lot easier from then on.

But, you know, I never mocked out another kid who couldn't do chin-ups. You know why? Because I knew how he felt. During those moments before I did my three chin-ups, I felt everything that the others, who weren't able to do any, felt; and I didn't want to inflict that kind of pain on anyone.

I'll never forget one day, when we were given a surprise spelling test. I stink at spelling and the aroma came through very clearly that day. The teacher read off fifty words, which we were to spell correctly. Then we exchanged our papers with a person next to us, corrected them, and read off the scores, so the teacher could record them. I handed mine to my best friend, who I thought would cheat for me, if I needed it. No such luck! The results were unbelievable: I got twenty-five wrong! *Half.* That was it. I was sick.

When my friend read the number to the class, the teacher asked for it again, because she thought it was impossible. "Twenty-five," my friend emphasized. The teacher was dumbfounded. It was the worst grade she had ever heard. She looked at me over her bifocals, and all she could say was, "Wow!" I think my friend was embarrassed to even grade the thing. He leaned over and said to me, "Man, you really stink!" No one in the room was more painfully aware than I was that I stank at spelling. My friend didn't have to tell me.

When you think about it, most mocking is drawing attention to the obvious. When the boy couldn't do a chin-up, our class must have told him a hundred times, "Ha, ha! You couldn't do a chin-up. You pip-squeak!" The whole time that poor kid was straining to do one, I'm sure he was saying to himself, *You pip-squeak!*

On the way to our next class, I can still remember my classmates coming up to me and asking, "Hey, Fred, you didn't really get twenty-five wrong on that test, did you? That's more than everyone else in the class put together." Boy, did they laugh at that one! And, boy, did I ever hurt. My mother could never understand why I studied my spelling so hard that next week.

The Pains of Nicknames

None of us knows how cruel we can be when we call people names, especially names that focus on a negative aspect of another person. The old saying, "Sticks and stones may break my bones, but names will never hurt me" is a pile of bologna. Names, especially with a pinch of sarcasm, hurt more than anything.

I used to do a lot of name calling, but I have since called several people to gain their forgiveness. Have you ever called another person by a less-than-complimentary nickname? Or perhaps you have been the victim of such abuse.

I knew a kid who was 215 pounds in second grade. He wasn't big—he was enormous! We called him the Crisco Kid.

There was a girl who would cry when she got nervous,

and, one day, she even wet her pants. We called her Sprinkler System.

A boy had slightly large ears. They weren't huge, but they were a little large. Well, we all noticed them, so we gave him the nickname Donkey Ears.

There was a kid in college who always hung around us. He never said a lot, but he would just always be there, so we called him Leech.

Another guy had one oversized tooth, right in the front. It was rather obvious, especially when he smiled. We called him Tooth, and, later, we started calling him Fang.

What do all these people have in common? They all had unique characteristics. And those characteristics became the trademarks and the titles of these people.

Pathetically, some people who get these subhuman nicknames put up with them, because they are at least known by something, even if it is a large front tooth. However, we will never know what deep pain we are causing these people, even though they might smile politely.

Mocking people or calling them by nicknames is usually slanderous. The word *slander* is defined this way: "to reduce a person to an object, to reduce someone to something, to make him less than human." It is no wonder that it hurts so much when we are mocked out or called by names. We know that we are human, and, as humans, we know that we are of value. And it makes us sad, and sometimes furious, when other people treat us as if we were subhuman. Such mocking can often have a highly destructive effect.

Janis Joplin, a female rock star of the late sixties, grew up in Texas as a cute, chubby girl with freckles. But, in high school, when her face was covered with pimples and her chubbiness turned to fat, her girl friends are said to have rejected her. She is said to have had an obsession with her personal ugliness. She tried to fit in and gain acceptance by being the buffoon, the brunt of the joke; but, the harder she tried, the more her classmates criticized her. Her peers laughed at her and made fun of her. They called her all kinds of names: Oddball, Freak, Pig. She would always laugh back, just to get along, but then she'd go home and cry.

After all the abuse and mocking she took in high school, she left Texas and drifted to San Francisco. She started to sing and drink. Her drinking turned into smoking pot, and from there she went into LSD and finally to "the big H," heroin.

Janis suffered greatly from self-hatred and insecurity. Her friends said that she couldn't spend a night without a partner. Finally, after a two-year lesbian affair, she was reported to be burnt out. To escape this futile cycle of pain, early one Sunday morning in October 1970, Janis Joplin was found dead, at the age of twenty-seven. The medical report showed that she died of an overdose of heroin. (*Time* [27 August 1973]:53–54. *See also Newsweek* 82 [29 August 1973]: 73; *Ramparts* 12 [7 November 1973]: 45; *Ramparts* 11 [3 July 1972]:50).

What the medical report did not show were the high-school friends Janis had, who caused some of the pain that drove her to such a pathetic death. Sticks and stones might have broken Janis's bones, but names hurt her even more: They broke something a lot more precious than bones— they broke her spirit.

Mocking and Compromise

A cutting remark can probably cause the most severe pain a person can feel. To avoid this, a lot of us are willing to do almost anything, even compromise our moral standards. The fear of what other people might say about you can get you to fall on your knees and cry out, "Hold it! I'll do anything! Just don't mock me out."

In the United States in 1976, an estimated one out of ten girls between the ages of fifteen and nineteen got pregnant. And a conservative estimate suggests that 50 percent of the girls between the same ages have had premarital intercourse. The figures run as high as 85 percent for males of the same age. In the seventies, an average of 200,000 teenagers per year gave birth out of wedlock. In fact, an appalling 30 percent of all babies born in New York City are born out of wedlock. (This statement does not even include an abortion rate of almost one out of two.) And in January 1978 the census bureau stated that there were 1 million unmarried couples living together in the United States.

My mind goes to those unmarried girls who are still virgins, and it cries out: *How are girls who want to maintain a high moral standard supposed to deal with the opposition?* I mentally strain, *How long can a girl be called a prude by her boyfriend, before she gives in? What can she do to avoid compromising?* When we think about the pain that is involved in maintaining a high moral standard, we can see why so many do compromise.

Drugs and drunkenness are other moral issues that face our youth culture. Federal health officials estimate that there are as many as 10 million problem drinkers or alcoholics in the United States. They blame drinking for 205,000 deaths per year. (*Time* [21 November 1977]:114). They estimate that 1.3 million kids between the ages of fourteen and seventeen have alcohol-related problems. (*Alliance Witness* [4 May 1977]:6–7). The other morning, as I woke up to my radio alarm, the news reporter stated: "Boston authorities say, 'Teenage drinking is out of control.' " I asked some friends of mine in a local New England high school how many of their classmates smoked pot regularly (a few times a week). They thought for a moment and said, "About eighty percent," and some thought higher.

Again, my mind goes to those kids who don't really want to get involved in drugs or alcohol, but who feel the pressure to compromise. I cry out, *How are they to handle the pressures to give in and light up a reefer (marijuana cigarette)? How many times can a kid be expected to say no to his friend who hands him a joint?*

It is no fun being slandered—being reduced to an object and being treated as something less than human. It is no fun to be called by a less-than-complimentary name. It is no fun when your friends mock at you or joke at you. In fact, all these hurt, and they hurt a lot. This pain is something we have all felt, and we will all feel again. The question is this: To compromise or not to compromise? It is very easy to squirm and avoid the pain by yelling, "Hold it! I'll do anything. Just don't mock me out!" But such a choice is a decision to compromise.

In the next two chapters, let's see what the costs of compromise are before we decide whether or not it is worth it. Perhaps there is a better way.

Feelings

1. Describe the first time you remember getting mocked out. Tell how it made you feel.
2. Have you ever had a nickname? Did it bother you?
3. What are some of the nicknames you have called other people? What would it feel like to be called by those names?
4. Have you been mocked out for being too straight? When?

Thoughts

1. Why are our reputations so important to us?
2. Why do we mock or tease others?
3. Do you know anyone in your school who might be like Janis Joplin? How do you treat this person?
4. What do you do when you're mocked out?
5. Which hurts more: sticks and stones, or ridicule from friends?

3
The Cost
Of Compromise

THERE ARE USUALLY 1,001 good reasons to compromise: "Everybody else does it. Why shouldn't I?" "It feels so good. And besides, nobody's perfect." "If I don't fit in, I won't have any friends." "Harvey has so many friends; I want to be like him." "If I don't do that, I won't get any dates." On and on the list goes. I have heard at least 1,001 very good reasons to compromise. In fact, I have used most of them. But the unfortunate thing is that most of us get suckered into believing these good reasons before we realize what it will cost us to compromise. Compromise is expensive. It costs more than anything else you will ever try to buy. Why? Because the decision to compromise may cost you your life.

Barbara is a very close friend of mine, but she has an alcohol problem. She comes over regularly, after school, to talk with Sherry (my dear wife) and me about a lot of things, but one day she was really upset with herself. "Life is a bummer," she started. "I am so sick of the way things are going. I just can't take it anymore."

Sherry and I listened very closely and tried to understand what she was feeling.

"I know what is right to do. I know that I shouldn't drink so much, but I just can't help it. I get around my friends, and they start drinking or dropping acid; and pretty soon there I go again." She breathed a long sigh and helplessly collapsed back into the chair. "I just hate it. I wish I could stand alone, but I can't."

Barbara was very honest with us, because she trusted us. She admitted that she couldn't do what she wanted to do—she couldn't be herself. She was caught by compromise, and it was costing her her life.

Compromise Is Hypocrisy

Compromise makes us hypocrites. Usually we think of a hypocrite in religious terms: someone who doesn't live up to his or her religious convictions. But Webster defines it this way: "One who plays a part; pretender; a person who pretends to be what he is not; one who pretends to be better than he really is . . . without really being so." By this definition, there are many different ways in which to be a hypocrite; there are athletic hypocrites, academic hypocrites, musical hypocrites, and social hypocrites. When a boy pretends to be the greatest football player since Joe Namath, his friends will call him "hot dog," but he is actually being an athletic hypocrite. He is pretending to be better than he really is. When Barbara got drunk, she was playing a part; she was trying to be different from the person she really was. She was being a social hypocrite, just to gain the respect of her friends.

Hypocrisy of Lying   Have you ever made a snowman? You start with a snowball about the size of a softball, and you put it down on the snow and roll it. You roll it until it's the size of a basketball, but nobody stops there! You roll it some more. And if you keep rolling it, it will get as big as you are. That's the way it is with lying. As Mark Twain once said, "The only difference between a lie and a cat is that a cat only has nine lives."

Nothing causes more lies than fears of peers. We want to impress our friends so much that we exaggerate the truth into a lie. Lying makes a perscn someone he or she is not. Therefore, every time we lie, we make ourselves hypocrites.

When I first met Tom, I really liked him. He was athletic. In fact, after I played tennis with him, I found out just how athletic he was. I immediately gained a lot of respect for him, and I wanted him to share that same respect for me. So I told him about some of my football experiences. The first few sentences, about being on the varsity team and starting on the offensive and defensive squads, were true. But he wasn't impressed, so I threw in a few more juicy stories.

Those stories sure were juicy. I even surprised myself with what a fantastic imagination I had. Finally Tom started to get impressed. The only problem was, what he really admired about me wasn't even true. I wasn't me. Webster's definition was true about me: "One who plays a part, pretender, a person who pretends to be what he is not; one who pretends to be better than he really is." I have since called Tom and told him the truth about those wild stories. When I finished he said, "Fred, I sure admire you for telling me the truth." I was fortunate and got myself out of a lie before things snowballed. George was not so fortunate.

I stood about eleven and a half inches taller than George. We both liked sports of all kinds; but the problem was that I would beat him at everything, because I was so much bigger. To make up for it, George would tell me about how much money his parents had and about everything they owned. For a while I believed him, because I knew they were very wealthy, but when he started to tell me about their helicopters and yachts, I knew he was stretching things.

One night, while eating dinner at George's house, his parents were discussing how they were going to travel to a nearby state. Without really thinking about it too much, I suggested, "Why don't you take your helicopter?"

They both sort of laughed, as if I had cracked a joke, and I laughed, too. George was the only one not laughing. He looked as though he were gagging on some peas.

"Is everything all right, George?" his mother asked.

He sat there in silence, bright red. Everything was fine physically; but things were not too good emotionally. George was caught in the snare of lying.

It's a funny thing, but looking back on George, the only thing I really didn't like about him was his lying. And yet that was the one thing he thought he had to do to impress me. But I didn't need impressing. I liked him already. He was afraid he had to measure up to me in some way in order to gain my acceptance and approval. But he was already one of my best friends. I liked George; the only thing I didn't like was when he tried to be someone else.

Hypocrisy of Living   Just about everyone has felt pressure to act differently from the way he or she is. The inner desire to find approval and acceptance by a certain group or by a certain individual can drive a person to do just about anything.

When I was a senior in high school, almost everyone was smoking grass. That is, almost everyone but Gordon and me. One night we were driving along with a bunch of our friends, on the way into New York City for the evening. Somebody in the front seat rolled a joint and lighted up. He took a toke and passed it. Everyone was smoking. "You smoke?" they asked me. "No, thanks!" I said, and a few guys chuckled. After a few moments of hesitation, Gordon said, "Sure."

The joint was passed, and the next thing we heard was an outburst of coughing. With tears rolling down his face and his body convulsing, Gordon attempted to clear his throat for quite a while. Everyone had a good laugh at Gordon. Soon his throat was clear, and it was also clear that he had never smoked grass before. For some reason, Gordon felt he had to be different from what he really was. He didn't like to smoke dope, but he compromised his standard and became the center of our laughter.

There was one boy in my school who was cruelly called Lizard, not because he looked like a lizard, but because he acted like one. He would just hang around with people. Whenever someone went to play Ping-Pong, he'd have to play Ping-Pong. Whenever somebody would go listen to records, he'd listen to records. And when he found out that we were all going out for the football team, he went out for the team, too.

It didn't take us long to realize that he wasn't a football player. After a few days of double sessions, he was thoroughly discouraged. The coaches showed him no mercy. They would throw him the ball and tell the rest of us to go tackle him. *Crunch!* I guess the coaches wanted to get him off the team.

Well, it worked. This boy quit the team, and, instead of going to practice every afternoon, he started going to the poolroom. Before long he became one of the best billiard players on campus. He found his thing. He didn't need football, and he also found that he didn't have to tag along with everyone else. He started to be himself, and he enjoyed it. Before long he even lost his nickname, Lizard, and he made a name for himself as a billiard player.

No one was born to be a hypocrite. When someone tries to be different from what he really is, or when he copies the behavior of others around him, he's actually saying, "I am afraid to be myself. If people know who I really am, I don't know if they will like me."

The real problem is this: Unless I decide to be myself, no one is going to like me, anyway. In fact, no one will ever know me—that is, the real me. If people like me just because of the lies I tell them about myself, then they are liking the fake me. This is a cost of compromise.

If I don't smoke marijuana, I should not fake it, just to impress others. If I do not have the potential to be a good football player, there is no reason to fake it. There are other things I can do. Trying to impress people by lying to them or acting cool will never get me what I really want. *Hypocrisy* is a dirty word. I don't know anyone who respects a hypocrite. Hypocrites are lonely; in fact, they are all alone because they are the only ones who know who they really are. Sometimes even the hypocrite himself forgets who he really is, and then he is in real trouble.

Compromise is costly. It makes hypocrites out of the best of us, and it costs us our lives.

Feelings

1. How do you feel toward people who lie?
2. Have you ever been caught lying? When? How did it feel?
3. Do you know anyone in your school who "tries to be cool"? Without naming him or her, describe the way this person acts.

Thoughts

1. What is a hypocrite?
2. Why do people brag and exaggerate the truth?
3. What is wrong with lying?
4. Why do people copy their friends?
5. Do you think it is risky to let people know who you really are? Why?
6. Do you have a best friend you can be yourself with? What is it about this person that makes him or her so special?

4
The
Crunch
of Compromise

YOU ARE A PART OF the do-your-own-thing generation that boasts of its originality. You claim to dress differently, cut your hair differently, play your music differently, and even talk differently from anyone else. Uniqueness and authenticity are the marks of excellence in this generation. You all want to be independent leaders—pacesetters. The kid who is the weirdest or the funkiest is "cool." And at times you even defiantly shake your fists at your parents, insisting, "I'm not copying my friends! I am just different from you!"

I used to insist that my generation was unique, too, but do you know what I say now? Bologna!

My mind was changed one day when I walked into McDonald's, and I took a look around at all the young people standing there. What I saw not only popped my bubble, but it almost brought tears to my eyes: everyone looked exactly alike—the same jeans, the same T-shirts, the same belts, the same hairstyles, the same shoes. I was crushed. I hated what I saw. We all looked the same, and suddenly I was struck by the ugliness of it.

I thought, *Why do we all look basically the same? laugh basically the same? listen to basically the same type music? and smell basically the same? How did we all get so much alike? Our do-your-own-thing generation is a flop!* The only reason everyone looks and acts funky is because funkiness is "in." But because everyone is trying to be different, nobody is *really* different from anyone else. I was disillusioned by what I saw that day.

Compromise Is Slavery

More than simply making us hypocrites, compromise can make slaves out of us. The day Barbara came over and said, "I wish I could stand alone, but I can't," she admitted she was a slave to her compromise. She had an alcohol problem that she couldn't deal with because she couldn't be herself around her friends. She had to compromise to be like them.

It is easy to want to be held or kissed or laughed with so much that we are willing to do anything. We can so much want acceptance by special friends that we cry out, "Hold it! I'll do anything you want. Just be my friend." Or, more impersonally, we can bow our knees to the crowd and cry out, "All right! I'll do anything; just let me fit in."

As soon as we cry out, "I'll do anything," we become prisoners to our own names. Our reputations and social acceptance become our masters, because we are willing to do anything for them. This bondage is stronger than steel and holds far more teenagers bound than chains or bars do. Part of the reason this bondage is so dangerous is that it is invisible, and it can hold us as prisoners without our even being aware of it. This is a cost of compromise. Think about it!

Compromise Is Death

The moment we start compromising, we begin to die, because we stop being ourselves—the persons God made us.

A good definition of sin is this: *Living in a way we were not intended to live.* We do this when we decide to compromise, and this is cheating ourselves and God.

The first creature who decided to live differently from the way he was intended to live was Satan. He was the first copycat. He wasn't satisfied with the way God made him, so he said, "I will be like God" (*see* Isaiah 14:14; 2 Thessalonians 2:4). The devil tried to copy the Person of God. One of the devil's most common tricks among teenagers is to get them to copy the behavior of others. He appeals to a person's jealousy and gets him or her to say, "I will be like _____."

If your best friend gets a new dress, you may say, "I will be like her," and you will go out and buy a new dress just like hers. If a boy steps up to bat before you and hits a home run, with thunderous applause ringing in your ears, you say, "I will be like him." A guy in homeroom gets a date with the homecoming queen, and other guys say, "Why can't I be like him?" So often we see others excelling in certain areas and we proceed to copy their behavior.

Paul described the game of follow-the-leader, which we so often play:

> At that time you followed the world's evil way; you obeyed the ruler of the spiritual powers in space, the spirit who now controls the people who disobey God. Actually all of us were like them and lived according to our natural desires, doing whatever suited the wishes of our own bodies and minds. In our natural condition we, like everyone else, were destined to suffer God's anger.
>
> Ephesians 2:2, 3 TEV

Paul shows here that the arch copycat is the devil; and when we march along, following the behavior of others, we are following in his train. We can be following along innocently for a while, but the Bible says, "There is a way which seems right to a man, but the end is the way to death" (Proverbs 16:25 RSV).

We were made unique. This means that, at day one, each of us was given all the ingredients to be at least partially different from any other person on planet Earth. Before you were born, there was no one exactly like you, and the day after you die there will not be another exactly like you. God intended each of us to be unique.

However, the moment you begin to copy someone else, you cease to be unique. When you start playing follow-the-leader, you start dying. Hence, copying others is a form of suicide. You are murdering your own uniqueness. Such death is an offense against God, because He made you, and you are telling Him that He did not do a very good job. This form of self-murder is indeed a sin.

Let's Be Honest About Ourselves

It was not easy for me to admit that I was being influenced by my friend. I could see other people being influenced by their friends, but I couldn't see it in myself. I was a high-school student who didn't want to be a follower. I insisted that I was my own person and that public opinion had little or no effect upon me. But, when I was a freshman, my dad told me I had to get my hair cut. I hated to get my hair cut. I liked long hair, and I just did not want to get it cut. Like most parents, mine did not like long hair, so my dad gave me two options: "Either go to the barber, or I will cut it myself." I thought it over and finally decided to let him cut it. What a mistake!

I can remember the event as if it happened five minutes ago. I sat in my room, where there were no mirrors, so that

I couldn't see the massacre take place. I took off my shirt and sat there, stiff as a corpse, with my eyes clamped shut. Snip, snip, snip—I can still feel every snip. It was like being awake during open-heart surgery. But, to a freshman in high school, he was cutting something more valuable than my heart: He was cutting my hair.

My dad kept trying to make conversation, but it was useless. I couldn't say a word, but I felt a great deal. When it was all over, he slowly, awkwardly, stepped from my room. Not knowing what else to say, he offered me these words: "Fred, I think you are being very silly about all this."

Several minutes later, when he was long gone, I rolled from the chair to my bed, stuffed my face into the mattress, and cried. I cried for a long time. Then, after I went into the bathroom and finally looked in the mirror, I cried a lot more—right through lunch and all afternoon.

Why did that hurt me so much? Why did I care what my hair looked like? At the time, I wasn't even aware of all my reasons. All I knew was that it hurt. To me, I just liked long hair, and that was "my thing." I was saying to my dad, "This may be the way the members of your generation cut their hair, but it's not the way the members of my generation cut their hair." Underneath the surface, in the subways of my heart, I was really asking the question, "Oh, no! What are *they* going to think about this ugly haircut?" I was concerned about what my friends at school would think.

Whether we choose to stick our heads in the mud and deny the influence of the crowd, or whether we admit to it, we are all touched by it. The desire for crowd approval has a subtle effect on all of us, and it is better to recognize it and deal with it than to deny its existence.

Sheep are said to be the most habitual animals known to man. They love to play follow-the-leader. A sheep will do whatever the other sheep are doing. Whole herds of sheep have been known to wander into disaster and even fall off the side of a cliff, because they were blindly playing follow-the-leader. It is no wonder that the Bible calls us sheep: "All we like sheep have gone astray; we have turned every one to his own way . . ." (Isaiah 53:6). Jesus wept for the people, because He saw them as sheep without a shepherd, and sheep without a shepherd do nothing besides follow the leader.

When we play follow-the-leader and do only what is safe and free from ridicule, we, too, might well wander off the side of some cliff and plunge to destruction. We need to be careful because the games we often play are dangerous.

Counting the Cost

By now, I am sure you realize that I hate the word *compromise*; compromise is the greatest single enemy of the human race. There is no more fatal disease known by God's people. All we have to do is adjust our convictions just enough so that they are no longer offensive to the crowd, and we have begun to die.

When I was in high school, I got sick of mimeograph paper. To this day, whenever I see that purple ink, I get sick to my stomach. We, as individuals, aren't supposed to be mimeographed copies, either. We shouldn't all look alike, smile alike, walk alike, talk alike, or even smell alike. When we start to copy the behavior of others, we stop being the unique individuals that God created, and to that extent we start to die.

Isn't there a better way of handling the opposition?

Feelings

1. Describe what it would feel like to be a slave.
2. In what ways do high-school students resemble sheep?
3. Is it easier to be yourself, or is it easier to compromise?

Thoughts

1. Why is compromise slavery?
2. Why is it hard to admit that we all copy other people's behavior at times?
3. Why is compromise death? Do you agree with this statement?

5
Christian Compromise

SCHOOL ISN'T the only place where you can be put in the clamps of compromise. In the church you can get pressured to act like a Christian, even if you aren't one.

Have you ever felt as if you were playing the great Jesus Christ-Look-Alike Contest? It is very easy to play. All you have to do is learn to say, "Praise the Lord!" wear a Jesus button or a cross; say grace before meals; read your Bible once in a while (but not too often) and go to Christian meetings now and then. Oh, yes! You must also have an emotional religious experience. Just raise your hand at an evangelistic meeting or walk the aisle in some church, and you are eligible for the contest.

There are as many hypocrites in church as there are in high schools. We can pretend to be such nice, moral kids and put in time at church on Sundays, while we live like hell every other day of the week.

False Christianity

The worst enemy of true Christianity is false Christianity, or Christian compromise. False Christianity is a disease that is easy to catch and almost impossible to get rid of. False Christianity spreads from person to person like the common cold, and yet it is as deadly as cancer. All you have to do is get injected with just enough Jesus serum to make you immune to the real thing. Karl Marx wrote, "Religion . . . is the opium of people." Unfortunately, this can be true, for a lot of people who have tasted nothing but fake Jesus serum. This kind of false Christianity is nothing but a narcotic used to avoid reality.

There are a number of ways false Christianity shows itself. Let's look at a few.

Evangelifish   Evangelifish are fake Christians who look a lot like Evangelicals, but are not the real thing.

Perhaps you have seen one of these creatures: They look and act a lot like a jellyfish.

Scientists tell us that jellyfish have no backbone and just drift along with the tide. When the tide comes in, they come in. When the tide goes out, they go out. They are 96 percent water, so when they wash up on the beach and are exposed to the sun, they virtually disappear.

Have you ever seen a Christian who just drifts along with the tide of public opinion? They are creatures with no backbone of their own so that when others around them are talking about Jesus, they don't mind talking about Jesus. But when Jesus is being mocked, they remain very silent. An Evangelifish goes up and down, according to whom it is with. In fact, when difficulties come along (when the sun comes out), some Evangelifish have been known to shrivel up and completely disappear. An Evangelifish specializes in compromise.

Fence Sitters   Fence sitters are another very common breed of fake Christianity. Perhaps you have seen them. They thrive in almost any religious environment, and they can be spotted straddling just about any fence.

A fence sitter has one foot firmly planted in the church and knows a lot about the Bible and scores very high on religious trivia. It can recite John 3:16, the Four Spiritual Laws, and the Lord's Prayer. It knows all the hymns and can pray along with the best of them. Usually a fence sitter was raised in the church and has been feeding on warmed-over Jesus material since it was able to eat. If the old saying "Familiarity breeds contempt" is true for anyone, it is true for the fence sitter.

Unfortunately, the fence sitter has another foot firmly planted in the world. Even though it is plagued by a long list of negatives such as, "Don't go to parties," "Don't smoke," "Don't listen to the radio," or "Don't swear when your grandmother is around," the fence sitter usually manages to get involved in more than enough trouble.

Having one foot in the world and one foot in the church, this creature usually experiences a lot of pain. It is also quite scary, because right underneath it lies the gaping mouth of the Grand Canyon, ready to catch its plunging body, if it takes a false step.

Jesus described such compromise when he said: "No one can serve two masters; for either he will hate the one and love the other, or he will be devoted to the one and despise the other. You cannot serve both God and mammon" (Matthew 6:24 RSV).

Fence sitters not only endure a lot of pain, but when they walk, they limp a lot, because of the bowlegged posture they maintain.

Chameleons A chameleon looks a lot like a real Christian, but it is a false Christian.

In the reptile world, a chameleon is a unique lizard that is able to change its color to match any of a variety of surroundings. Christians with this particular disease are very hard to spot, even though they are very common, because they are able to blend in so nicely anywhere. They make it their habit not to stand out on any issue and refuse to be controversial or offensive. They are willing to compromise at the blink of an eye.

Chameleons exist if you can find them, in almost any climate. They do very well in church buildings, pot parties, discos, evangelistic rallies, nude beaches, and so on. But you do have to look for them, because they don't stand out. They are not known for anything exceptionally good. In fact, they are hardly known at all.

If you should spot one, you have no reason to be afraid of it. It's harmless. Just be careful that you don't begin to copy its behavior, or else these words of Jesus might be true about you, too:

> You hypocrites! Well did Isaiah prophesy of you, "These people say they honor me, but their hearts are far away. Their worship is worthless, for they teach their man-made laws instead of those from God."
>
> Matthew 15:7–9 LB

Common Disease of Christian Compromise

What do Evangelifish, fence sitters, and chameleons have in common? They are all varieties of the common disease known as fake Christianity; in fact, these are so common that genuine Christianity is hard to spot.

The other day I was walking along, and I looked up at a cross on the top of a building. It stood up very tall, silhouetted against the sky. Then a mockingbird flew by and landed very near the cross. As I stood there and thought about it, I was amazed at the symbolism. How many mockingbirds land near the cross and pretend to sing its song, only to get up and fly somewhere else and sing another song!

There are a lot of Jesus Christ look-alikes in the world today. Paul described these people as ". . . preferring their own pleasure to God. They will keep up the outward appearance of religion but will have rejected the inner power of it. Have nothing to do with people like that" (2 Timothy 3:4, 5 JERUSALEM). Therefore, we need to be sure that we are not just mockingbirds.

The ABCs of Not Knowing Jesus

The mockingbird knows only three notes: *A*, *B*, and *C*. *A* stands for "activities, *B* for "beliefs," and *C* for "companions." Each note is necessary for the mockingbird to be able to make its familiar tune.

A: Activities   It is very easy to be involved in a lot of nice, religious activities—Sunday school, church, youth group, prayer meetings, Bible studies, choirs, and so forth—and never know Jesus. When we get involved in Christian activities, it is very easy to fit in, without ever knowing Jesus. Activities don't save us.

B: Beliefs   Have you ever hiccupped your way through a sermon? It is easy to do. Just sit in the pew, eyes transfixed on the pulpit, and mumble to yourself, "Yup! Yup! Yup! Yup!" all the way through the sermon. Do not challenge anything. Do not raise any questions, and do not even think. Just sit there passively and hiccup: "Yup, yup, that's right! Yup! Yup! Yup!"

Certainly there is nothing wrong with belief. In fact, without believing in Jesus, it is not possible to be a Christian. But, while it is true that we are saved by faith, it is possible to passively know the right things without having living, active faith. The Bible says that simple head knowledge is worthless: "You believe that there is one God. Good! Even the demons believe that—and shudder" (James 2:19 NIV). One can have the Christian hiccups and know the right things, but never really know Jesus.

C: Companions   We can have very moral, Christian friends and yet not know Jesus personally. Jesus said that He will separate the sheep from the goats (*see* Matthew 25:31–33), but today we are all walking around together. It is very easy for a goat to walk around with sheep long enough to learn to sound like a sheep: "Baa! Baa! Praise the Lord! Baa!" A goat will even start to smell like a sheep if it hangs around with the flock long enough. It is possible to hang around with Christian friends and to have good, clean Christian fellowship and yet not really know Jesus.

There are the ABCs of the mockingbird. Unfortunately, mockingbirds only copy and do not have an authentic tune of their own.

The Secret Christians

Evangelifish, fence sitters, and chameleons are all Jesus look-alikes, but they are not Jesus people. However, there is another person who might actually be a genuine Christian but who has his or her own disease: He or she wants to live like an undercover agent, like a Jack-in-the-Box Christian. People like this have put their faith in Jesus alone for their eternal salvation and are actually indwelt by the Spirit of God, but the fact that they are genuine Christians is the best-kept secret they have.

Undercover Agents (Jack-in-the-Box Christians)   All week long, an undercover agent keeps his born-again head in his born-again shell, like a turtle—until Sunday morning, when he goes *pop*, and out he comes, singing hymns and smiling and even closing his eyes with everyone else—only because things are safe and the coast is clear. Then, after the evening service he goes home, tucks himself into bed, pulls the covers over his head, and falls asleep, thinking about how different things will be in his Monday-morning classes. And so, life goes on for the undercover agents week in and week out.

Undercover agents are hypocrites: They are hiding their true identity as children of God. The undercover agent lives in fear of his friends' reactions if they were ever to find out that he was actually a genuine Jesus person. Undercover agents are caught by the fear of peers, and they are afraid to stand alone. Undercover agents refuse to tell the truth about themselves, for fear of rejection, and they find it much safer to travel incognito. Undercover agents are more concerned about the applause of men than the applause of God; they are more concerned about "what will *they* think" than "what will *He* think."

Lukewarm Vomit

Everyone mentioned in the past few pages has one outstanding characteristic: Each makes God sick to His stomach! God's stomach gets sick when He observes an

Evangelifish drifting along with the tide of public opinion. He cannot stomach fence sitters with their bowed legs—one in the world and one in the church. He notices the chameleon changing its colors depending on whom it is with. And God gets nauseous when He sees a child trying to play the game of undercover agent. All of these are forms of Christian compromise. Each is a particular variety of fake Christianity that God cannot swallow. Someday they will form one big puddle of lukewarm vomit (Revelation 3:16).

Christian compromise is very costly.

Feelings

1. Can you identify with this chapter? How does it make you feel?
2. Have you ever met any fake Christians? Describe their traits.
3. Have you ever felt pressured to "act Christian"? In what ways?
4. What would it feel like to be an undercover agent?

Thoughts

1. How would you describe false Christianity?
2. In your own words describe the following:
   a. Evangelifish
   b. Fence sitters
   c. Chameleons
   d. Mockingbirds
   e. Undercover agents
3. Which variety of false Christianity is the most common?
4. Why would the people mentioned in this chapter make God nauseous?
5. Compare false Christianity to genuine Christianity.

6
Made To
Be Me

WHEN THE CROWD CRIES out, "Do it our way!" we can either give in to its pressures or say, "No thanks! I'd rather do it my way."

We are well aware that any deviation from the norm is dangerous: We might get mocked out or get fed to the lions. Sometimes the crowd will even come right out and say, "Hey, you can't do that! *Nobody* does that. You have to get in line and play follow-the-leader, like the rest of us."

When such an attack comes, you are faced with this decision: Should I compromise or should I do it my way?

The other day, when I was driving along with one of my best friends, he told me about how he got sick of the pressures to compromise and decided to do it his way. He is a junior at a local high-school campus. He plays guitar and keyboards in a Christian rock group and has written a number of songs. He also plays basketball and tennis, and academically he is number one in his class. I asked him, "Hey, Scott, have you always been as outgoing as you are now?"

He looked over at me as if I should have known better than to ask such a stupid question. "No way! I used to be one of the shyest kids in junior high. I used to spend a lot of time alone; I would read for hours and spend even more time by myself, shooting baskets."

"How come?"

"I just didn't have any real friends. Kids made fun of me because of my good grades."

I was shocked and didn't know what to say. After a few moments, I asked, "What was it like to live like that?"

"Well, it was hard," Scott said. "I felt so much pressure to be like everybody else, but I knew that I couldn't be. I didn't want to smoke pot. I didn't know how to dance. I lived a lot in my own mind, in my own imagination—in a sort of fantasy world. Now, when I look back on it, I can't believe how much time I spent in my own thoughts. I felt really alone."

I knew that Scott was telling me something very important to him, and I respected him for being so honest. Most of us aren't that honest with ourselves, let alone with our friends.

"Well," I asked, "what helped you change to be the way you are now? You are so outgoing and confident!"

"Oh, that's easy! When I met Jesus, for the first time in my life I was able to love myself. It really helped me when I realized that Jesus felt my pain. He felt the pain of rejection. He knew what it meant to be kicked around, just like me."

I was hanging on every word.

"Then, when I felt His love and acceptance, I was able to accept myself. I didn't have to be someone I wasn't. I figured that, if He could accept me the way I was, I might as well accept myself. I guess it means a lot to me, too, that He created me. If He made me, I must be okay, right?" I can still see him beaming as he told me this.

He continued, "When I opened up my heart to His love, He actually set me free. I can't exactly explain it, but He set me free from my self-consciousness. He even set me free from my boredom and loneliness. And most of all, He let me love myself. I just praise Jesus that He loves me."

Scott knew what it was like to be bound by the chains of peer fear. He knew what it was like to be mocked, and he felt the pain of critical remarks. He spent a lot of time alone and retreated into a world of his own. But, rather than compromising, he found another alternative. He found that he could be himself. And, soon after he accepted himself, his friends at school began to accept him, too.

Jesus Felt My Pain

Lee Harvey Oswald was a lonely teenager—he never knew that Jesus felt his pain. He was raised by a very dominant mother, who showed him no affection, love, or discipline. His friends at school had little to do with him, and at thirteen, his school psychologists said he didn't know what it meant to be loved. The girls teased him, and the boys beat him up. As an escape from all the abuse, he joined the marines, but only found more abuse there. They called him Ozzie the Rabbit, which he hated, so he got in a lot of fights, rebelled, and finally was court-martialed and dishonorably discharged from the marines.

There he was, without family, friends, and love. He was losing his hair, and had no skill or self-respect.

He eventually married an immigrant, who bore him two children. But soon, even his marriage—the only source of security he had ever known—began to crumble, and his wife hated him. Having lost all self-worth, one day he crawled to her, begging, with tears, that she show him some attention. In front of his friends she mocked his failure and ridiculed his impotence.

Finally, his ego lay shattered, and he was without any human affection at all. A few days later, November 22,

1963, he went out into the garage, took a rifle, drove into Dallas, and put two huge holes in the head of our former president, John Fitzgerald Kennedy. (James Dobson, *Hide or Seek*. Old Tappan, NJ: Fleming H. Revell Co., 1974).

Lee Harvey Oswald knew no love or affection. All he knew was the severe pain of a shattered ego. He felt the stinging mocks from his early childhood through young adulthood. Psychologically, he was shell-shocked from all the abuse. So, without any fame, respect, popularity, or beauty, he rose to kill the most respected, the most popular, the most "beautiful" person on earth.

What would have happened if this tragic person had known that Jesus felt his pain? What would have happened if Lee Harvey Oswald had known that Jesus loved him personally? What would have happened if Oswald had known that Jesus was despised and rejected, a man of sorrows, and acquainted with grief? If he had known this, he might well still be alive—and so might John F. Kennedy.

Scott was kicked around, too. Kids laughed at him and mocked him. Scott felt a lot of pain. He used to come home from school, pull out his basketball, and shoot hoops, because he felt safe doing that; he was free from the attack of his friends at school. He was so mocked and kicked around that he felt more comfortable when he withdrew to be by himself.

After a basketball game in which Scott had been a high scorer, he thought, *At least now they will finally accept me!* As they all ran into the locker room, his teammates gathered around Scott, but instead of cheering him, they shoved him and poked at him and abused him more than ever. He was punched in the face and slapped around. Then someone said, "Go home, Scott! Brains don't play basketball." When Scott went home, he was wounded. He felt the pain of rejection by his friends, and he knew what it was like to be alone. He hated it.

How was Scott able to deal with all those bruises? He met Someone who was bruised even more than he was: He met Jesus. And Scott realized that Jesus wasn't anything great to look at either; that He wasn't Mr. Personality or some "beautiful person"; that He was actually mocked out, kicked around, and spat on; He was called by more nicknames than most of us (like Prince of Satan and Sinner and Glutton and Drunkard); that He was rejected by every one of His close friends. He was a total social reject: people actually couldn't stand to look at Him, and they slapped Him in the face and pulled out His beard; even as His body dangled from the cross, dripping tears and blood, and as He sucked the last few mouthfuls of air, the crowd was still screaming, "Come on, you turkey—compromise!" When Scott realized that Jesus, the Second Person of the Trinity, actually experienced all the same pain he felt, Scott felt loved. Scott realized that Jesus knew what it felt like to stand alone and get mocked. In fact, Scott realized that Jesus went through all that trash just so that we might be able to see how much God loves us and how much He understands our pain.

There are many different kinds of pain we can feel. Every year, 2 million more kids discover that their parents are getting divorced—and that hurts. (*Boston Globe* [7 November 1978]). A sociologist at the University of Rhode Island has estimated that an additional 2 million children are physically abused every year. (*Boston Globe* [21 November 1978]). They are kicked, bitten, punched, beaten, stabbed, and, at times, even shot. There is an estimate that in the city of Boston there are 40,000 kids who have been sexually assaulted before they reach their sixteenth birthdays. (*Boston Globe* [27 September 1978]). All such child abuse hurts. It is no wonder that every night so many kids fall asleep crying.

The teenage years are full of pain. Much of the pain is caused by adults, and some is self-inflicted. Grief is caused by mocking mouths in locker rooms and jesting tongues in the hallways. But, regardless of the cause, we all need some way to deal with pain.

Have you ever been kicked around and spit at by a mocking, jesting gang of friends? It hurts! But if you have felt this distress, I have good news for you: Jesus felt your pain, too. He is God, and He felt everything you felt. Even more than that, He can be with you and help you handle it.

He Accepted Me

After Scott realized that Jesus felt his pain, he didn't have to worry about hiding from the kids at school anymore, because he was comforted by Jesus, the God-man, who felt everything he'd ever felt. Scott was able to open up to himself and others. Despite the fact that Scott's friends rejected him, Jesus accepted him. Scott found in Jesus a real friend—Someone with whom he could be himself, Someone whom he could always trust, always talk with, and always count on.

Did you know that Jesus accepts us? When we think about all the times we have blown it, all the times we have hurt other people and hurt ourselves, it is really hard to believe that God accepts us. When we think about the pain we have caused our parents and about the laws we have broken and all the garbage we have gotten ourselves into, it is hard to believe that God is still holding His hands out to us. But He is. The lyrics of Jamie Owens' Collins song are God's words to you:

The Father's Song

If you could see deep inside of Me,
You would cry and reply with an open heart.
If you could reach to the depths of Me,
You'd find your pain and the strain of each tear you cried.

How many times I have longed just to hold you
And protect you from the pain the world can give;
But you run ev'ry time I get near you,
Can't you see I want to teach you how to live!

If only once you would look at Me
Through the eyes of a child who has lost his way;
Then you would know you could come to Me
To be fed and be led safely home to stay.

How many times I have longed just to hold you
And protect you from the pain the world can give;
But you run ev'ry time I get near you.
Can't you see I want to teach you how to live!

In a world full of rejection and pain, God says, "I know what you are feeling. I know what you are going through. I know how easy it is for you to get down on yourself. I know what it is like to be rejected. (People reject Me all the time.) In fact, I know what it is like to be rejected by *you*. But I still love you and accept you right where you are."

When I was in high school, I had a girl friend whom I

really liked a lot, but she didn't know Jesus. Her life was pretty messed up. She was into dope pretty heavily and had a lot of problems at home. I wanted her to come to know Jesus. So I decided to invite her to a Billy Graham Rally. To my surprise, she accepted.

We went into New York City on a bus and filed into Shea Stadium, along with thousands of others. We got good seats, and she seemed to be really getting into it. Graham preached a real zinger, and I could tell that she was really touched. When the invitation was given, she sat there and didn't move.

I was a little disappointed, so, on the bus, on the way home I asked her, "Do you want to give your life to Jesus?"

She looked at me very seriously and said, "I would love to give my life to Jesus."

I got so excited. "Well, would you like to pray with me? You can do it right now."

"Fred," she explained, "I would love to give my life to Jesus, but I am too messed up. Maybe someday, when I am forty-five and married, after I get all my wild desires out of me, I can go to a Billy Graham Crusade and walk down the aisle and meet Jesus. I'll be able to straighten my life out by then." It really hurt me to hear her say those words. I did everything I could to convince her that she didn't have to clean up her life before she could come to Jesus, but she didn't believe it.

This happened over eight years ago, and as far as I know, she is still waiting to clean up her life. If you are like this friend of mine, please don't wait any longer. Please, do not say, "I'm too messed up." Jesus specializes in messed-up lives. Some of His best friends have been alcoholics, prostitutes, thieves and murderers.

God wants you to hear Him say, "I love you just the way you are. Don't change yourself. Just come as you are." Jesus accepts you. The question is: Do you accept Him?

When Scott learned Jesus accepted him, he felt love. For the first time in his life, he was able to say, "Jesus, if You can accept *me*, why shouldn't I accept *You*?" Besides accepting God's love in Jesus, Scott was able to accept himself.

Despite the fact that Scott's friends rejected him, Jesus accepted him. Scott found in Jesus a real Friend, someone with whom he could be himself, someone whom he would always trust, talk with, and always count on.

Did you know that Jesus accepts you just the way you are? Did you know that you aren't expected to clean up your life before you can come to Jesus? Jesus loves you just the way you are. He is a genuine Friend, and He wants you to know Him personally.

God Made Me

Scott also realized that God created him. Today we have dozens of reasons not to believe God created us. Scientists suggest that there is a survival of the fittest among animal life and that natural laws of evolution brought man into being; this theory robs humanity of personal value and dignity. With the dramatic and tragic upswing in abortions (one out of two, in some cities), we are all aware that we, too, could have just as easily been aborted. With all the violence we observe in our society, it is very easy to lose sight of the value of life. Statistics show that the average high-school senior has seen 18,000 murders on T.V. It is no wonder that H. Rap Brown said, "Violence is as American as apple pie." So much of our society is saying, "Life is cheap," that it is an easy lie to believe.

This is part of the reason why there are so many ĸids in our country who want to die. There are three times as many youth suicides today as there were twenty years ago. Every year there are an estimated 400,000 youths who attempt suicide, and 100,000 succeed. Among people between the ages of fifteen and twenty-nine, the only cause of death which exceeds suicide is car accidents. This means that if you are going to die in the next few years, the chances are quite good that you will kill yourself.

Time magazine carried an article entitled, "Children Who Want To Die," which described cases of child suicide. A boy eight years old hanged himself. The article contained the results of a survey taken of 127 children. An amazing 41 percent of them admitted to having thought about suicide.

As I think about these figures and the state of many kids around our country, I fall down on my knees and cry out, *Oh, God! What is lacking! What do the kids need to hear to convince them that they are valuable? that life is really worth living?* The words come back, *Tell them I created them and that they are of great worth to Me.* Let those fourteen words reverberate in your brain a thousand times.

This is why one of the wisest men who ever lived said, "Remember also your Creator in the days of your youth, before evil days come, and the years draw nigh, when you will say, 'I have no pleasure in them' " (Ecclesiastes 12:1).

Another way of putting these words is to say, "Hey, teenager, before you start saying to yourself, 'Why don't I commit suicide?' remember that God personally created you."

When Scott took this advice and remembered his

Creator, he realized that he was not a clone or the strictly biological product of nature, but that he was actually the personal handiwork of God. He was able to accept himself. He was able to say to his Creator:

> You made all the delicate, inner parts of my body, and knit them together in my mother's womb. Thank you for making me so wonderfully complex! It is amazing to think about. Your workmanship is marvelous— and how well I know it. You were there while I was being formed in utter seclusion! You saw me before I was born and scheduled each day of my life before I began to breathe. Every day was recorded in your Book.
>
> Psalms 139:13–16 LB

Scott learned to love the person God made him, regardless of what others thought. Even though his friends at school still laughed at him for different things, Scott was able to accept himself, because he knew that he was God's workmanship (Ephesians 2:10).

God wants you to know that you are of great value to Him. He wants you to know that He made you to be the person you are and that, because He made you, you are beautiful, regardless of what anyone else thinks. Jesus loves your smile and the shape of your nose. He loves your hair and your size and shape. He loves you, even when you do not love yourself.

The Missing Ingredient

It is impossible to copy our way into the Kingdom of God. Acting like Christians does not make us Christians any more than acting like trees in a school play will actually make us trees. That is impossible! The only way to be a tree is to be born as a tree, and the only way to be a Christian is to be born again.

I was talking with Scott, and I asked him how he actually became a Christian. He smiled and said, "Well, I was raised in the church and went to Sunday school all my life, but I realized that I was missing something. Things were dull and boring, but I didn't know why. As I thought about it, I knew that what I was missing was Jesus."

He went on to illustrate: "I was sitting on my bed one day, and I looked over at my transistor radio with the earphone sticking out of it. I could turn up my radio as loud as I wanted, but I wouldn't hear anything. I could know everything about that radio—how to take it apart and put it back together again. But until I stuck the earphone in my ear, I couldn't hear the music. That's just the way it was with me and Jesus. I was wired for sound, and I knew everything about Him, but there was no music, until I stuck Jesus into my life. And then, *wow!* did I ever hear the music."

Scott's life was boring and dull. Sitting through sermons was like trying to eat sand. All he could do was to copy the outward behavior of those he thought were Christians, but there was nothing real about it. He was playacting. Then he realized that he could know Jesus firsthand.

Scott said he talked with Jesus: "I said, 'Jesus, I know a lot about You, but I don't know You. I am sick of tagging along with the Christian crowd. Right now, come into my life and take it over. Make me the person You created me to be."

You know what happened? Jesus did it! Jesus started

living in Scott, and at that moment Scott was born as a Christian. He didn't have to worry about acting like a Christian anymore. Now he *was* one! Scott went from wallowing in the puddle of lukewarm vomit to swimming in the fountain of life.

Have you ever accepted Jesus? Have you ever opened your heart to His love and let Him come in and fill you with peace and joy? Why not talk with Him right now about it?

To Compromise, or Not to Compromise

Scott was able to stand against a lot of criticism and feel a lot of pain that told him to compromise, but he said, "No, thanks, I'd rather be me." I have seen his life change over the past few years. He is now one of the most respected kids in the school. Once he learned to accept himself as the person God made him, he became more acceptable to others. The deep, genuine friendships Scott craved several years ago are now his because he dared to be himself even when the crowd was saying, "You can't do that!"

No one is born a copy. We are all born unique. Once we die there will never be anyone exactly like us. When we look at someone at school whom we really respect and try to copy his or her behavior, we are playing follow-the-leader, and we are failing to live up to our full potential. The problem is this: You can't look at any person and find perfection. This is the difference between us and machines. There is a model Honda that all Hondas are to look like, and unless all the pieces fit together just perfectly, it will not run properly. Even a peanut-butter-and-jelly sandwich needs to have just enough peanut butter and just enough jelly. But people are different. There just isn't a right way to laugh or a perfect way to talk. You can't find a model hairstyle that everyone should have. How boring! We need to maintain our individuality. This means we need to learn how to say, "No compromise!"

If you have felt a lot of pain and have been criticized a lot because you are being the person God made you, then let the fact that Jesus felt your pain touch you where it hurts. If you have been kicked around and rejected, don't think you're alone in your pain. Jesus is there with you, and He knows what it feels like.

If you have been suckered into compromising and have followed the leader into a lot of muck and garbage, don't think God has given up on you. He hasn't! If your life resembles the local junkyard (full of accidents, useless material, and disregarded pieces) don't think that God sees you that way. God accepts you. He wants you to come home. He wants you to know that His arms are open wide and that you don't have to change your life around before you come. If He accepts you, don't you think you should accept yourself?

If you have believed the lies that life is cheap and your life is insignificant, allow the words of God to echo in your brain, when He says, "I made you." Everyone you have ever known may have told you that you aren't worth a Bic pen. Just this once, let God tell you, "I made you." And even though no one may ever have asked you to do something so difficult, try to believe that you are loved so much by God that He gave His only Son for you.

Your life is unique and I hope God keeps it that way. Please, don't let the crowd squeeze any life out of you by putting you in the clamps of compromise.

 # Feelings

1. What makes kids feel like committing suicide?
2. Do you think God really knows what it feels like to get mocked out?
3. Did you ever feel as if you were too "messed up" to be a Christian? Why do people feel that way?
4. What would it feel like to run from God? Why do people run from God?
5. What did it feel like for Scott to finally become a Christian? Have you ever felt that way?

Thoughts

1. Have you ever thought about suicide? When? Why?
2. Why did it make a difference to Scott when he realized Jesus felt his pain?
3. Why did Jesus hang around with prostitutes, gluttons, and alcoholics?
4. Does God intend Christians to be unique? If so, in what ways?

7
Will You Dance With Me?

A CHRISTIAN is not a copy. In fact, a Christian cannot be a copy. A Christian has got to be an original.

When God invites us to be called by His Name—*Christ*ian—it is like being invited to dance when we have never danced before. It is a totally unique experience. Ken Medema is a blind musician who wrote a song about learning to dance with Jesus:

> Well, He asked me to dance,
>   and I'd never tried dancing before.
> I had visions of saints and angels
>   laughin' us right off the floor.
> No, I protested,
>   it just wouldn't be any good.
> He gently insisted, and
>   finally I told Him I would.
>
> Unforgettable, well, He was the coming
>   of Spring on a cold winter's day.
> Unforgettable, for He taught this singer
>   to sing in a whole new way.

Jesus talked about dancing. He said:

> To what, then, can I compare the people of this generation? What are they like? They are like children sitting in the marketplace and calling out to each other. "We played the flute for you, and you did not

dance; we sang a dirge, and you did not cry.' For John
the Baptist came neither eating bread nor drinking
wine, and you say, 'He has a demon.' The Son of Man
came eating and drinking, and you say, 'Here is a
glutton and a drunkard, a friend of tax collectors and
"sinners."' But wisdom is proved right by all her
children."

Luke 7:31–35 NIV

The crowd cried out to John the Baptist, "Dance for us!
Come on! We're playing you a tune!" But John the Baptist
had on his heavenly earphones and was tuned in to WGOD.
He wasn't about to do the Taiwan Two-Step for the crowd
when he could dance for His Creator.

John was obedient. He left his family and friends to go
out into the wilderness and preach the Gospel. He hated
sin and even spoke out against the king's adulterous relationship. He was so radical that the people called him a
madman and finally sent him to the chopping block, to have
his head cut off because he refused to compromise. The
crowd wanted John to join their chorus line, but the Bap-
tizer was listening to the heavenly channel. It is not surpris-
ing that Jesus said of John, "I tell you, among those born of
women [which includes all of us] none is greater than John
. . ." (Luke 7:28). John was a God pleaser, not a man
pleaser or a woman pleaser.

Jesus did the same thing. The crowd screamed at Him,
"Hey, You can't dance like that! Nobody dances the way
You do. Come on, we're playing a nice worldly waltz for
you, and we're not quite sure what to call that thing You're
doing." But Jesus had His heavenly earphones on, too, and
wasn't about to miss a step.

Our problem is that we are so used to seeing people look alike and dance alike that when God comes along and asks, "Will you dance with Me?" we are not sure what to say. We know God is going to have us dance a little differently, but we are not sure if our friends are going to be able to handle it.

You Can't Dance With Chains On

I think the number-one reason why high-school students do not publicly follow Jesus is because they are afraid of what their friends will think. Those four words *What will they think?* form the question that goes through most minds that are deciding whether or not to follow Jesus. Those four words are like chains around our legs; they keep us from dancing.

Marsha came up to me, sobbing, after one of my talks at a youth retreat. "I want to live for Jesus, but I just can't," she cried.

"What do you mean, 'I can't'?"

"Well, I just can't," she sniffled. "I mean, nobody else does." She went on to tell me about her past. "You see, I gave my life to Jesus two years ago. I mean, I really gave Him everything. I don't do anything part way, and when I became a Christian, Jesus was everything to me. He was so real. I loved Him so much!"

I nodded and began to understand.

"I went to school, and I told all my friends about Him. I mean, I told everybody, whether they wanted to hear or not. A couple of friends even came to church with me, and they ended up becoming Christians, too. But then every-thing went bad."

She cried, and I told her I knew how she felt, because I

went through high school as a Christian, too. As I listened to her, it was as if we were tuned into the same channel.

She continued, "My friends ended up mocking me out at school and calling me names like 'Jesus Freak' and 'Fanatic,' and they kept telling me how much fun it was to go out and have sex with the guys. Even the kids at church weren't really into Jesus. They were into a lot of fun and games and socials, but not Jesus. You see, I really wanted to live for Jesus, and I tried." She sniffled some more. "But I can't, because it's too lonely."

"Marsha," I said, "I think that, perhaps for the first time in your life, you are really dealing with what it means to be a Christian." She started to dry her tears and looked at me as if my head had suddenly turned into a tomato. "No, I am serious. A lot of people are running around saying, 'God is like Coca-Cola: "Things go better with Jesus." ' But you are finding out that that is not always the way it goes."

She nodded, because she knew there were hard times.

"Jesus said, 'If anyone would be My disciple, he must deny himself, pick up his cross and follow Me.' Right now you are faced with that decision. Are you going to follow Him under those conditions?"

"Yeah, you're right. That is exactly where I am, but I just don't know what to do." She paused and then added, "It is so hard to stand alone. I just don't know what to do."

As I listened to Marsha, I could feel her struggle and confusion. My heart hurt so badly. It was as if someone were doing open-heart surgery on me—with a chain saw. With every cell of my body, I wanted her to follow Jesus; but I could feel the struggle she faced. I could hear the tune of her friends at school playing like a broken record in her brain. And I could hear the tune of God playing in the background. There she sat, with her face in her hands, bowing beneath the burden of guilt.

"Marsha, I wish I could make things simple and take away the demands Jesus has placed upon you, but I can't."

She nodded and accepted my concern.

More than anything, I didn't want her to lose heart, so I asked her a question I already knew the answer to. "Do you love Jesus?"

She nodded her head, "Yes."

"Do you trust Him?"

Again she nodded, "Yes."

"Do you trust Him with your eternal life?"

"Yup!"

"If you trust Him with your eternal life, do you think you can trust Him with your reputation?"

A little smirk rose from the corner of her lips.

"You know that a Christian is someone who trusts in God alone to save her eternally, because of what Jesus did on the cross. Well, a Christian is also someone who trusts God with her reputation. Christians trust God with their popularity. After all, isn't it a little strange to trust God with our eternal lives and yet not trust Him with our temporal lives?"

"When you put it like that," she said, "I guess I don't really trust Jesus, do I?"

The last time I looked into Marsha's eyes, she thanked me for being honest with her and for seeing through the mask she was wearing. She told me I was the first one who had ever been so honest with her. Because I was touched by her hurt, I have prayed for her dozens of times, even though we'll probably never see each other again until the Judgment Day.

You might be smacking your lips and criticizing Marsha because of her weakness. I don't! I respect her! She felt the cost of following Jesus—that it involved trusting Him with her reputation—and she struggled deeply with it.

There are thousands of Marshas bound by the same chains of peer fear on every campus. You know, it's hard to dance when you've got chains on. The problem is, most of us aren't willing to be as honest as Marsha was.

There is no way any of us can follow Jesus, unless we are able to trust Him with our reputations. Unless we can trust Him with our names, He is not going to gladly share His Name with us. There are thousands of students all over the world who have decided to be better friends with the crowd than with Jesus. God says to those in this category:

> You are as unfaithful as adulterous wives; don't you realize that making the world your friend is making God your enemy? Anyone who chooses the world for his friend turns himself into God's enemy.
>
> James 4:4 JERUSALEM

What a rebuke!

Nothing New

Peer fear is nothing new. In fact, our parents have to fight it as much we do. You might hate the Bible, but please allow me to show you an example of adults who were bound by peer fear so much that they couldn't even speak:

> Yet at the same time many even among the leaders believed in him. But because of the Pharisees they

would not confess their faith for fear they would be put out of the synagogue; for they loved praise from men more than from God.

John 12:42, 43 NIV

If those words didn't grab you around the neck, go back and read them again.

The synagogue used to be the social club; it was the school, the church, the corner store, and the Friday-night disco club, all thrown into one. If you were put out of the synagogue, you were a total social zero. These verses show that in Jesus' day there were people who saw and heard Jesus and even believed in Him, but who would not admit it publicly, because they were afraid of their friends: fear of peers. These adults were actually hypocrites; they were compromising what they really believed, just so that they could fit in with the status quo. They were more concerned with the question, "What will my friends think?" than what Jesus was thinking.

I don't care who you might be—the quarterback on the football team or a freshman girl with a bad acne condition—we all have asked ourselves the question, "What will my friends think?" Most of us have probably thought about following Jesus, and some of us might have even gotten saved, but right at the point where it really counted, we compromised and said, "Yeah, I hear the voice of God calling me, and it sure sounds like the beat of a drum I have never heard before. But if I start dancing to this new rhythm, I'm going to stand out and be different from everyone else—and, after all, that's risky!" Have you ever said anything like this, either by your words or actions? If so, you might have believed in Jesus, but you have not followed Him. In other words you can't be an under-cover agent for Jesus. He said:

> So every one who acknowledges me before men, I
> also will acknowledge before my Father who is in
> heaven; but whoever denies me before men, I also
> will deny before my Father who is in heaven.
>
> Matthew 10:32, 33

Repent

The first word on the lips of John the Baptist was *repent* (Matthew 3:2). The first word on the lips of Jesus was *repent* (Matthew 4:17). The climax of the first Christian sermon ever preached, at Pentecost, was *repent* (Acts 2:38).

What does it mean to repent? It means "to dance to the beat of a different drum." It means that we go from asking, "What will *they* think?" to, "What will *He* think?" It means we stop playing follow-the-leader and start following the Leader. It means we go from the fear of men to the fear of God. It means we stop living for the applause of men and start living for the applause of God. It means we go from saying, "The crowd is Lord," to saying, "Jesus is Lord."

Have you ever repented? Have you ever made the changes I have just mentioned? Have you ever decided to stop dancing like a clown before the crowd and start dancing with your Creator? Have you ever decided to follow Jesus?

T. S. Eliot was questioned about his Christianity, and he said, "To a generation that is running away from reality, one who is moving toward it will seem like a deserter." This great American poet was right on target. The first thing that we all realize when we turn to follow Jesus is that we are dancing to the beat of a different drum.

As Larry Norman sings:

"Two roads diverged in the middle of my life,"
I heard the wise man say.
I took the one less traveled by
and it's made the difference every night and every day.

Excerpted from "One Way" on Larry Norman's Solid Rock album, IN
ANOTHER LAND, SRA 2001 distributed by Word Records.

My friends, it will make all the difference in your life if you
take the road less traveled by, even as Larry Norman did.

The Final Question

Since we all need friends, and since our reputations are
very important to us, the ultimate questions are these: Can
I trust God? Does He really have my best interests in
mind? If I become a Christian, won't I be committing social
suicide and become the cockroach on campus? These are
the questions that keep students from following Jesus. We
are afraid that, once our friends find out we are followers of
Jesus, they will cease being our friends.

This is where God calls on His children to have faith.
When Jesus calls a high-school or college student, He says,
"If you really believe in Me, then trust Me with your repu-
tation."

When Jesus invites us to become Christians, He invites
us to dance, and that means publicly. He doesn't want us
dancing in front of our mirrors in the privacy of our own
rooms.

Patti is a senior in high school, and she is dating a Christian guy who used to shoot cocaine through his veins, before he met Jesus. She loves Jesus and has taken a very
definite stand as His follower. She has decided not to com-

promise. She and I were talking the other day about her relationship with her boyfriend.

"Oh, things are going great," she said. "They couldn't be better."

"Well, you have such a high moral standard. Don't you have any trouble with that?"

"Oh, no. Andy is a Christian. So we both want to stay pure until we're married," she explained. "The only problem I have had was with my best friend. She kept telling me, 'You have to have intercourse with Andy. My boyfriend and I do it all the time. You wouldn't believe what a rush it is!' This went on for weeks, and finally she told me she couldn't be my friend anymore."

"Wow," I was really feeling with Patti. "How did that make you feel?"

"Oh, I felt terrible—like a klutz. It seemed as if a knife went into my stomach. I was numb." She thought for a second. "Then, after a while, I felt such a strong love for her, and I realized that she needs Jesus forever, and my hurt would only last for a short time. I knew how important it was for her to see me as a friend of God."

I was really amazed at how mature her thoughts were.

"And, besides, I know that if our friendship is worth anything, we will be able to handle this."

Patti is a girl who has repented: She has gone from dancing before the crowd to dancing with God, and she has trusted God, even with her reputation. She has counted the cost, and she has even had to pay for it, but she has decided not to compromise. She would rather even temporarily lose a friend than make herself an enemy of God.

I have never met Keith Green, but I love him. His music has been a great inspiration to me, particularly his album *No Compromise*. On the album jacket, he writes:

NO COMPROMISE is what the whole Gospel of Jesus is all about . . . 'For I tell you . . . no man can serve two masters . . .' (Matt. 6:24). In a day when believers seem to be trying to please both the world and the Lord (which is an impossible thing), when people are far more concerned about offending their friends than offending God, there is one answer . . . Deny yourself, take up your cross and follow Him! (Luke 9:23).

He sings a song his wife wrote, entitled, "Make My Life a Prayer to You." Read it through a few times. Think about what it feels like to say those words. Think about some of the chains that might be keeping you from dancing. And if you can handle it, make these your words as you talk with Jesus.

> Make my life a prayer to You
> I want to do what You want me to
> No empty words and no white lies
> No token prayers, no compromise
>
> I want to shine the light You gave
> Through Your Son You sent to save us
> From ourselves and our despair
> It comforts me to know
>   You're really there
>
> I want to thank You now
> For being patient with me
> Oh it's so hard to see
> When my eyes are on me
> I guess I'll have to trust
> And just believe what You say

Oh You're coming again
Coming to take me away

I want to die and let You give
Your life to me that I might live
And share the hope You give to me
The love that set me free

I want to tell the world out there
You're not some fable or fairytale
That I made up inside my head
You're God the Son
You've risen from the dead

Feelings

1. What would it feel like to stand up in front of your schoolmates and tell them you love Jesus?
2. Describe what it would have felt like to be John the Baptist when:
   a. He rebuked King Herod for his adulterous relationship
   b. He left his family to go out alone in the wilderness
   c. He saw people respond to his preaching
   d. He finally saw Jesus himself
   e. He found out he was to be decapitated
3. In your own words describe the tension Marsha felt.
4. Would you say it is easy or hard to live for Jesus in your college or school? Is it worth it? What are the pluses and minuses?

Thoughts

1. What made John the Baptist so unique?
2. What does it mean to repent?
3. Be honest: When you have thought about following Jesus, have the words, *What will they think?* gone through your mind? Why?
4. Is it easier to trust Jesus with your eternal life or with your temporal reputation?

8
Friends

I READ THIS in the newspaper the other day:

On the morning of Tuesday, January 10, 11-year-old Linda Ann Herman [name changed] complained of a stomachache to her sixth grade teacher at the . . . Elementary School. Excused from school shortly before noon, Linda walked less than half a mile to the . . . Methodist Church, entered the front door, and seated herself in the second pew from the front.

Some time during the next two hours, Linda took a .38-caliber pistol, pressed it against the center of her forehead, and pulled the trigger. She died instantly.

Many of the mourners at the funeral three days later were children, classmates of Linda's. None, however, had been close to Linda because she was a child without friends.

I don't care who you are, you can't live without friends. Friends are to people what ink is to a pen or what water is to a plant. You can't live without friends.

It mutilates my heart to think about Linda Ann Herman, and thousands of others like her, who want nothing more than a best friend, but don't even know where to look. Very few of us know how to recognize a friend, even if we see one. And fewer of us know how to be a friend.

Fake Friends

Most of us want to have friends so badly that we are willing to do almost anything to get them. Hypocrisy, bragging (lying), and compromise are all too often a part of making friends. We want to have friends so much that we might "act cool," tell exaggerated stories, or even lower our moral standards to impress others. There is only one problem: It is impossible to make genuine friends this way. All you end up with are fake friends.

Who are fake friends? Fake friends are people who always smile at you. Fake friends talk a lot about themselves. Fake friends are people who never disagree with anything you say. Fake friends will mock out their other friends when they are with you—and they will probably mock you out when you are not around. Fake friends are afraid to stand alone and will usually go along with just about anything; they specialize in compromise. Fake friends get up and leave when you blow it. Fake friends will do a lot to impress you. Fake friends will lie. In fact, fake friends find it necessary to lie, because they just aren't satisfied with who they really are. Fake friends are fake, and there sure are a lot of them.

Only
Honesty Is the ~~Best~~ Policy

If you think about who your best friend is, I would imagine that someone will come to your mind with whom you are able to be honest. Who is a friend?

A friend is someone who will tell you when you have bad breath. A friend is someone who will listen to you when you get really ticked off. A friend is someone who will argue with you for hours. A friend is someone who hates the way you comb your hair, but puts up with it, anyway. A friend is someone with whom you can be yourself. A friend is a swift kick in the pants. A friend likes you enough to tell you the truth. A friend will keep a secret. A friend will sit next to you on the bench after you've struck out. A friend is hard to find. In fact, you will be a wealthy person if you find three of them in your whole lifetime.

When I was in sixth grade, none of the guys would admit to liking the girls. For seven years of grammar school we had put a great deal of pressure on each other to "hate 'em." If anyone admitted to liking a girl, he was mocked and ridiculed to the point of tears.

I can still remember the night I was sipping Coke at Roger's house, after our baseball game, and he asked me, "Who do you like in our class?"

I couldn't believe my ears. There I was: *Should I lie?* I thought. *I surely can't tell him who I like!* But then, I thought about Roger and what a faithful friend he was, so I got up enough guts, and I told him, "I like Cathy."

Wow! What a feeling of freedom and release. After seven years of secrecy, I finally admitted to one of my friends that I really liked a girl.

Roger went on to be my best friend because he never told anyone my secret. And before that night was over he even told me who he liked. The only problem was, it turned out that he liked Cathy, too!

It is so easy to hide behind masks and keep secrets from each other. It is easy to get trapped by wanting to make such a good impression that we act "cool." We so want to be accepted that we fail to be natural and honest. We desire reputations so much that we will fake and lie and compromise to get them. But after a while, we find out that it won't work. It is impossible to make real friends by hiding ourselves. If we fake it, the only thing we will gain is fake friends. If we put on a show to impress others, they might like the act we are putting on, but they won't like us. In fact, they won't even know us.

Making friends starts with the two words *no compromise!* The only way we are ever going to make friends is to allow people to know who we really are. And the only way people are going to know who we really are is to be honest and possibly make ourselves vulnerable. The only way to make a friend is to say, "Here I am! Take it or leave it." Friends are those special people we can trust enough to be honest with them.

Standing Alone

It might seem contradictory, but the only way we are ever going to be able to make genuine friends is to be willing to stand alone. Until we have gotten to the place where we are willing to stand alone on moral issues, even if it means losing friends, we are not ready to make friends. If our friends will cease being our friends because we hold to certain standards, then they were not our friends to begin with. And if our friends like us only because of the way we compromise, then our friends are only fake friends.

In high school I had two best friends: Jerry and Tod. We did everything together. We went to concerts together. We went to classes together. We ate lunch together. We taught Bible studies together. Basically, when we did anything, we did it together.

One weekend they went out hitchhiking, just to get away. On Monday morning they came up to me, beaming with excitement, to tell me about their weekend. After they hilariously slapped me around for a while, they were able to say more than expletives.

"We found a rodeo tent," Jerry explained. "So we got jobs. Man, you wouldn't have believed it! We made two hundred dollars, and they gave us wine—all we could drink! And you wouldn't have believed the girls—foxes, every one of them! So, the last night there, we grabbed the wine and took the girls out into the woods."

I was hurt. Rather than relishing their excitement, I couldn't believe what I was hearing. For the first time in my life since I'd met Jesus, my friends were looking at me nose to nose, expecting me to drool over their folly.

"I don't want to hear any more," I told them.

They were silenced. Their mouths were empty. "Come on, Tod, let's get going. Fred must be tired. We'll see him tomorrow." And they left.

That hurt. It really hurt. They were my best friends, and we had spent countless hours together. Suddenly it all seemed to be gone. *What should I do?* I thought. *Am I just being self-righteous? Should I laugh with them over the fun they had, even though it was sinful? What if they don't like me anymore? What if I lose my two best friends?* All those and many more questions went through my mind. Although I sincerely enjoyed their friendship, the sorrow in my heart caused by their sin was something I could not deny.

We avoided each other for a week; but, finally, it was unavoidable. We had to talk. So we sat down in one of the buildings at school. I had decided I wanted to love Jerry and Tod. I was not going to judge them, because I knew that I sinned a lot, too. But if they were going to reject me because I was a "prude," then I would have to accept their rejection.

"Fred, I just can't handle you anymore," Jerry started in. "You are just too straight. I just can't live that way. Once in a while I want to go out and get drunk and have some sex. Life is too short not to have fun."

I sat there silently, feeling everything he said.

"You can live straight if you want to, but it's not for me."

We must have talked for an hour, but we didn't get any further. Finally Jerry said, "Fred, you are right. You are living for Jesus, and God is using you. Maybe someday I will get my life turned around, but for now I just want to live free and have fun. I don't see any way that we can be friends anymore."

Jerry got up and walked away, and Tod went with him. I was left there, all alone. Losing those best friends was like starting high school all over again. It was like being locked out in a blizzard, without any clothes on. It wasn't cold; it was freezing! I wanted nothing more than a genuine friend, who would accept me; but I knew that I had to be willing to stand alone. Compromise might have gotten me a companion, but it would never get me any friends.

(By the way, Tod stopped by to see me a few years later to tell me that he got sick of the way he was living and went to talk with his pastor. That day, Tod met Jesus, and he wanted to let me know about it. As Tod walked out of my room, I thought, *What if I had compromised? What if I had lowered my standards?* I would have felt like a guilty fool. I was glad Jesus kept me faithful and that Tod knew that I still loved him.

When Tod left, he said something like, "Fred, thanks for being a faithful friend." Those two words, *faithful friend,* echoed in my brain for a while. All I could say was, "Praise the Lord!" After Tod left, I got down on my knees and thanked Jesus for teaching me how to say, "No compromise!" Only Jesus was able to make me a faithful friend.)

A Friendship Is a Trust Company

It is impossible to have friends unless we have the courage to make ourselves vulnerable. Unless we are willing to risk being hurt, mocked, taken advantage of, or fed to the lions, we aren't willing to make friends.

When I was in sixth grade and told Roger that I liked Cathy, I was petrified, because I felt I was risking my life. Nobody admitted that he liked a girl. But I took the risk because I trusted my friend. And that night, when I told him, he told me whom he liked, and we became best friends. We formed a trust company.

Keeping secrets makes friends, and every time we tell someone a secret, we are taking a risk. But, after all, a friend is someone we trust. So, with a friend, there really is no risk and no reason to fear the outcome of what we have entrusted to him or her. There is no fear of peers with friends. "A friend loves at all times. . ." (Proverbs 17:17), even when your hair is in curlers, after you've flunked a test, or during the big game in which you play "left out."

In the Bible, it says:

Love contains no fear—indeed, fully-developed love expels every particle of fear, for fear always contains some of the torture of feeling guilty. The man who lives in fear has not yet had his love perfected.

1 John 4:18 PHILLIPS

Hank was a boy who felt more than his share of pain in high school. He was tall and skinny. His classmates used to tease him that on Halloween he should take off all his clothes, put on a turban on his head, and go around as a Q-tip. Hank was not only thin but his skin was also the color of milk; and his red, curly hair shadowed his face. He was not at all athletic and didn't do anything after school, except play with the computer.

There were a bunch of Christians in his class who got annoyed with all Hank's classmates who mocked him out, so they decided to do something different. Someone suggested, "Let's love Hank." They all agreed, "Yeah, let's be his friends."

Hank had never gone out on a date in his life, so some of the Christian girls started to call him up. After school they took him to Burger King for a Coke. Our youth group was going to a pro basketball game, so the guys asked Hank to come along with us, and he accepted. We even fought over who would ride in his car.

It took Hank a long time to trust them, because he had never in his whole life trusted any of his peers. It took Hank a while before he was able to accept their friendship; but, after several months Hank started to respond. He started showing up at our meetings, and then he started asking questions. It wasn't long before he met Jesus.

Hank never had friends before, because no one ever accepted him for who he was. But a few kids decided to change all that. They decided Hank was worth loving, and they did everything they could to prove that to Hank. The result was that every particle of fear evaporated from Hank's heart, and he was able to trust his new friends.

They formed a trust company that was worth more to Hank than all the oil in Iran. They made friends.

Please Be My Friend

Do you have a friend? Do you have someone who will accept you for what you are, even when you're not so hot? If you do, you are a wealthy person. But, if you don't, you are like most people.

In 1970, a survey was taken of 7,050 high-school students, who were randomly selected from various groups around our country. The results, reported by Merta P. Strommen in *Five Cries of Youth*, showed that a large number were haunted by thoughts of failure and self-criticism. "They compare themselves with people who excel in an area," the report stated. And they ". . . remain preoccupied with standards and the task of making it in the eyes of others."

This obsession clearly shows the bondage of fear that is caused among students by the quest for a genuine friend. This fear of peers needs to be dealt with head-on. As W. C. Fields has said, "There comes a time in the affairs of men, my dear blubber, when we must grab the bull by the tail and face the situation." If your social life resembles the hind end of a cow, don't worry about it. Most of your friends' social lives look the same way. However, you might be hearing a different tune in the air. You might hear your Maker calling out to you. You might hear Him trying to explain that He felt your pain and that He accepts you just the way you are. You might even hear Him inviting you to be His friend.

"No compromise" is the heart of the Christian message, because it is the most important message every human needs to hear. Compromise is slavery and death. People are literally dying to hear those words: *no compromise.*

To be willing to stand alone and to say, "No compromise," is to say, "God made me this way. I'm sorry if you can't handle it. But if you can handle it, you can be my friend."

The crowd is waiting for someone to say, "No compromise," because every member of the crowd is looking for a friend who will accept him and yet be himself.

Almost two thousand years ago, Jesus started a movement of no compromise. Hallways, classrooms, cafeterias and locker rooms are filled with imposters. But Jesus is still the same. He doesn't compromise. When He hung on the cross, He said, "No compromise." When He rose from the dead, He said, "No compromise." Today He is seated on the throne of God, and He rules the universe, saying, "No compromise." Some day you and I will be kneeling before that throne, and we will be judged by whether or not we said, "No compromise."

God invites us to dance to a new rhythm, and He warns us by saying:

Do not model yourselves on the behaviour of the world around you, but let your behaviour change, modelled by your new mind. This is the only way to discover the will of God and know what is good, what it is that God wants, what is the perfect thing to do.

Romans 12:2 JERUSALEM

If you can, have this little talk with Jesus:

I have heard You call my name, and I know that I'll never be the same. I have felt Your love, and I know that You care for me. You made me, and I guess I can trust You with my reputation. You know how important it is to me, so please take good care of it.

I want to be the person You have intended me to be. Forgive me for copying my friends, for compromising my standards, and for doing what I knew was wrong. Take away my guilt, because it's killing me.

You know how weak I am when I try to stand against the crowd, so be strong in me. Help me say, "No compromise." Help me obey You, because I want to stop playing follow-the-leader and start following You.

Show me how I can be a friend, and won't you please give me a true friend: someone I can trust, someone I can be myself with, someone who will see me just the way I am and like me anyway.

Lord Jesus, thank You for being my Friend and for teaching me that there's nothing wrong with saying, "No compromise." You are my example, and I want to be just like You.

Jesus, I love You.

Jesus is a friend because He is totally honest and totally consistent. He said, ". . . I will never fail you nor forsake you." (Hebrews 13:5). He said, ". . . I am with you always. . ." (Matthew 28:20). Jesus is not going to walk away when you are cut from the tennis team, or when you fall off your skateboard, or when you flunk a math test. Jesus is not going to leave when you sit home the night of the prom, or when you wake up with a big red zit on your chin, or when you drop the pass in the end zone. Jesus loves you, and He promises to be closer than a brother.

Jesus knows there is nothing more important to most of us than having a close friend. This is why He first offers us His friendship and then He shows us how to make friends.

As the Bible says, "There are friends who pretend to be friends, but there is a friend who sticks closer than a brother" (Proverbs 18:24). This is the kind of friend we all want, and this is the kind God wants us to have.

Feelings

1. Describe how Laura Ann Herman felt. What would it feel like not to have any friends? Have you ever felt that way?
2. Describe what it feels like to have a friend.
3. Is it easy for you to be honest at school? Why or why not?
4. When Jerry and Tod came back after their wild weekend, how would you have responded, if they were your friends?
5. Do other people's sins ever hurt you? If so, when?
6. What does it feel like to stand alone? Give an example of a time when you have had to stand alone.

Thoughts

1. Why is it impossible to make friends by compromising?
2. Why is it hard to make genuine friends?
3. List five characteristics of a genuine friend.
4. List five characteristics of a fake friend.
5. How can you be a better friend?
6. Why do secrets strengthen friendships?
7. Could you call Jesus "my best friend"? Why or why not?

9
Get Out
Of Your
Diving Bell

I WANT YOU TO HANG on to your chair tightly as you read this next chapter, because I don't want anybody to get wiped out. I have written this chapter with great fear, because it has a highly explosive content. I feel as if I'm stirring a nitroglycerin cocktail. If you can understand what I'm trying to say in these pages, you might be one person through whom God can change the world. But if you misunderstand what I am saying, your life might be destroyed. So, please proceed with caution.

HAVE YOU EVER gone to school feeling as though you were in a diving bell? Once we decide to follow Jesus and uphold a moral standard, we can feel so separated from our friends that we think we no longer have anything in common with anyone. We peep out our portholes and wave at people as they swim by, but we are afraid to get close to anyone. We are so afraid to catch any diseases, that we can totally isolate ourselves from others, and live all alone in our very own sterilized diving bells. We can get so paranoid that we actually expect people to chase us with butterfly nets and haul us off to the local kennel! These feelings of alienation are perhaps the most harmful feelings a young Christian can have.

Christian Withdrawal Is Not Christian

Often our schedules get so filled with Christian activities that it is enough to make us sick: Bible study on Monday night, discipleship training on Tuesday, prayer meeting on Wednesday night, choir practice on Thursday, hymn sing on Friday night, Christian fellowship on Saturday; and, of course, we spend all day Sunday at church. Everything on the schedule is all very religious, but this is not Christian. Total withdrawal from the world is not even healthy.

I went over to Gloria's house one afternoon because I knew that she had a bad case of the blues. Gloria is a very popular girl, and she likes to have a lot of fun; so when she got down, I was a little concerned.

After we talked for a while, I casually asked her, "What did you do last weekend?"

"I baby-sat for the Smiths."

"Well, what are you doing this weekend?"

"Oh, I don't know. I guess I'll just stay home and watch TV, as usual.

Suddenly, things became very clear to me. It was obvious that Gloria's social life had shriveled up like a dead frog.

"Have you been doing anything with your friends, after school, this week?" I asked.

"Nope, I usually just come home and study, and then I'm off to work."

"Well, who's your best friend these days?"

"Ann, I guess, but she smokes marijuana now, so I don't see her very often."

"How often do you get together?"

"The only time I see her is at school. You know, we have some classes together." Then she added, "My parents don't want me to get too worldly. And since I really want to obey God, I just don't want to be around my old non-Christian friends anymore. They can have a bad influence on you— you know?"

Gloria loved Jesus, and she thought that the best way to stay pure was to go to school in a sterilized diving bell and wave to her friends through the portholes, as they swam by in the miry sea of pagan society. The only time she would emerge was when she was baby-sitting or doing homework. She wanted to live a holy life so much that she didn't want to get close to anyone at school, because she thought she might catch some sort of spiritual Legionnaires Disease. When I recognized what was happening, I knew I had found the source of her blues. I went on to talk with Gloria about the importance of being *in* the world without being polluted *by* the world.

So often when we try to deal with the negative influences of the crowd, we think we have to withdraw—to break off all contact with the world and hang around with Christians all the time. And when we have no close Christian friends, then we just have to be alone, bite the bullet, and bear it. This, however, is not what God says.

I told Gloria, "God never asks any of us to be islands. He doesn't expect us to withdraw from our non-Christian friends. In fact, Gloria, one of the biggest problems we can ever have is when we twist the command, 'Be ye separate,' into meaning, 'Don't hang around with.' God wants us to hang around with non-Christians. He never asks us to physically separate ourselves from non-Christians, *except* when we are weak in a certain area. What He does ask us to do is to live a different life-style than our friends."

We went on to talk about this for almost an hour, and she was full of questions. The whole thing was new to her, and she was actually scared by it. She even said, "It's a lot easier to withdraw from my old friends than it is to hang around them anymore." And she added, "It might be easier on me, but I know that it is not healthy."

First Get the World Out of You

Worldliness is not an external thing. It is internal. Jesus never said, "Get out of the world," but He says, "Get the world out of you!" There is nothing wrong with having non-Christian friends. In fact, there is something pathetically wrong if we do not have any. Jesus had all kinds of them. He hung around at the local pub with the town boozers. He spent time with prostitutes, and some ·of his best friends were involved in organized crime (tax collectors). The problem comes when we start copying the behavior of others. That was something Jesus never did.

Winkey Pratney, a mouthpiece for God, who loves Jesus and loves students, has said, "Change your conduct or change your name." Those of us who follow Jesus bear the name *Christian*, and we are supposed to live up to that name in our personal conduct.

Free love (free lust) is as plainly forbidden in the Bible as adultery and murder. "God's plan is to make you holy, and that means a clean cut with sexual immorality" (1 Thessalonians 4:3 PHILLIPS). In a day in which there are far fewer virgins than nonvirgins, it is hard to believe that even arousing lustful desires is plainly forbidden by God (Matthew 5:27–30; 2 Timothy 2:22). We all need to decide that we are not going to compromise our moral standrards in the area of premarital sex, even if it means losing friends or dates.

Drunkenness is as plainly forbidden in the Bible as adultery and murder: ". . . be not drunk with wine" (Ephesians 5:18 KJV). In New York City, it is estimated that at least 60 percent of the kids between the ages of twelve and eighteen use alcohol regularly, and at least 36,000 have drinking problems. The Gallup poll shows that, in the United States, in the four years between 1974 and 1978, alcoholism increased by 50 percent (*Alliance Witness* [31 May 1978], :31). In 1976 the Minnesota Council on Alcohol Problems reported there are 1 million teenagers in the United States with drinking problems and 450,000 between the ages of ten and seventeen who are alcoholics. (*Alliance Witness* [4 May 1977]:6–7). This is tragic!

If drunkenness from alcohol is forbidden in the Bible, certainly the high caused by marijuana, hash, pills, or other chemical drugs is also forbidden. Besides, all such drugs are illegal, and God plainly forbids outlaws (Romans 13). In such a day, when you feel totally strange at a party, if you don't sip a little Bud or tequila, it is hard to believe that no drunkard will get to heaven (1 Corinthians 6:9, 10 Galatians 5:21). If we decide to go to parties, we first need to decide that we are not going to compromise our moral standards in the areas of drinking or using drugs, even if it means losing friends.

The Bible as plainly forbids rebellion against parents as it does adultery and murder. "Children, obey your parents in the Lord, for this is right. Honor your father and mother." (Ephesians 6:1, 2). In a day in which, "Independence is next to godliness," it might be difficult to believe that God really expects us to do what our parents say. But we all need to decide that following what our parents have to say is more important than doing what our peers tell us is good.

Shoplifting and vandalism are as plainly forbidden, in the Bible, as adultery and murder. "Let the thief no longer steal, but rather let him labor, so that he may be able to give to those in need".(Ephesians 4:28).

The FBI reported, in 1976, that vandalism in schools in the United States cost us $600 million, and there were 70,000 teachers assaulted. In New York City alone, there are an estimated 200,000 kids who stay home from school every day (*Time*, "Youth Crime Plague" [11 July 1977]:20). There are approximtely 80,000 youths sentenced to juvenile prison every year, and over 1 million more are put in jail. (*Youth Today* [September 1975]). In Washington,

D.C., a six-year-old boy siphoned gas out of a car, poured it on his sleeping neighbor, struck a match, and watched the man sizzle. (*Time* [11 July 1977]:19)

In such a day when it is "cool" to break laws, God still says it's wrong. We need to decide that we are not going to shoplift anymore and even pay some stores back, even if none of our friends understand why.

Witchcraft, astrology, seances, "white" magic, T.M., and other cultic-demonic activities are as plainly forbidden, in the Bible, as adultery and murder. "Shut out from the city shall be the depraved, the *sorcerers*, the impure, the murderers, and the idolaters, and everyone who loves and practices a lie!" (Revelation 22:15 PHILLIPS, italics mine). In a day of so many self-appointed gurus and fake messiahs, it is hard to believe that there is still only one way. No matter what our friends are doing, we need to decide that we are not going to look for our own personal demons through any of these spiritual counterfeits.

Secular rock music is not as plainly forbidden, in the Bible, as adultery and murder, but listen to what Mick Jagger, of the Rolling Stones, had to say about it:

> Too many people are becoming obsessed with pop music. The position of rock and roll in our sub-culture has become far too important, especially in the delving for philosophical content.

Donovan said, "Pop is the perfect religious vehicle." (Jonathan Eisen, ed., *The Age of Rock* (N.Y.: Vintage Books, 1970), pp. 338, 339). Frankly, I like music with more beat to it than a lot of the funeral dirges they play in some churches, but we need to be humble and honest enough to recognize that a lot of the doctrines of demons that have been exposed are being communicated through the medium of secular rock music. God says, "Don't let you A.M. radio squeeze you into its mold, but let Me remold your minds from within" (*see* Romans 12:2).

I realize that I have only mentioned a few moral issues we need to be faithful in upholding. I have not tried to make a complete list. I have only intended to mention some of the obvious, outward, behavioral examples of moral issues.

If you are involved in any of those areas briefly mentioned, I appeal to you as a child of perhaps the final generation: Repent from these godless life-styles and start dancing to the beat of a different drum.

Jesus gave His friends a prediction. He said, "In the last days, wickedness will be multiplied and most men's love will grow cold" (*see* Matthew 24:12). I think those fifteen words are being fulfilled today. Never have people been so wicked and yet so proud of it! Our country is glorying in its shame, like a pig in the mud. If ever the followers of Jesus were called on to be different, it is today. If ever we need to learn how to say, "No compromise!" it is today. Here is a short prayer I suggest that you memorize: "Do thou, O Lord, protect us, guard us ever from this generation" (Psalms 12:7).

In spite of the fact that Jesus knew it would be very difficult to stand against the crowd in such an evil day, He said to His Father, "I do not pray that thou shouldst take them out of the world, but that thou shouldst keep them safe from the evil one" (John 17:15). He doesn't tell us to get out of the world. That is the easy way. He tells us to get the world out of us, and then He calls us into the world.

Then Get Into the World

Once we have established definite moral standards that we will keep, even if it means losing friends, we need to hear Jesus' urgent call, "Get into the world" (*see* Matthew 28:19). If we have constructed some sort of diving-bell apparatus that helps our fears and insecurities, we need to break out of it.

C. T. Studd, a wild man for Jesus, wrote:

> Some want to live within the sound
> Of church and chapel bell.
> I want to run a rescue shop
> Within a yard of Hell.

Too many of us hide from non-Christians, as if we were undercover agents. Someone has said, "We are like the Saint Lawrence Seaway—frozen at the mouth." As Christians, we should not isolate ourselves, but infiltrate the world.

I had just started a discipleship group for high-school- and college-age students, and I was hoping Sharon would be a part of it. I saw her at the pool, so I asked her if she was interested.

"I have prayed a lot about it," Sharon said, "and I would love to come; but I am not going to."

I was crushed.

She saw my smile fall off my face, so she explained, "I am sorry to disappoint you, but you see, I don't have enough time to be with my other friends, if I am involved with too many meetings all the time."

Wow! I thought, *she has it together more than I do.* I

know that her "other friends" were non-Christians and she did not want to isolate herself.

"I am too involved with the clubs at school to be doing things with the church *all* the time."

Sharon was right. She knew that it was more important for her to build relationships with her friends than it was for her to go to another meeting.

Someone has said, "We can get saved in the church, but we become Christians in the street." Sharon knew the importance of Bible study, prayer, and worship; but she also knew the importance of a balanced life with her friends at school. She had to guard her schedule from getting too filled with church-related activities so that she could be active on campus. Once Sharon got the world out of herself, she knew that it was time to get herself back into the world.

Peter used to smoke a lot of pot, and he dropped some acid from time to time. Then he met Jesus, and for one year he knew that he should not go to parties, because there would be too much temptation to fall back into his old way of life. Then, after much prayer and Bible memorization, he decided he would attend them once in a while to keep up his relationships with his friends. At times, Peter was tempted to hit up, so he had to leave the parties. But he has not fallen to the temptation, and he has had a lot of opportunitites to share Jesus with his friends.

Once, a very close friend of Pete's, with whom he used to drop acid, began to really nag at him to do some dope. What was Peter going to do? Would he compromise? lower his standards "just this once"? Or would he stand up for what he knew was right? Peter battled with the temptation, but finally he said, "No! Jesus has set me free from having to get wasted, and I love Him too much to disappoint Him." Peter remembered the words of Solomon, "My son, if sinners entice you, do not consent. If they say, 'Come with us' . . . my son, do not walk in the way with them, hold back your foot from their paths" (Proverbs 1:10, 11, 15).

Peter knows his weakness and has committed himself to *no compromise* in the area of drugs, and he has also committed himself to being in the world as an infiltrator. Such a position is genuine Christianity—to be in the world but not of the world.

Getting Involved

To be in the world is to feel the pains of our friends: to share the hurt of a friend who has divorced parents, to pat the back of a friend who was cut from the team or who lost the school election, to sit next to the kid who always eats alone in the school cafeteria, to talk to the fat girl who is never asked out on a date. School is a place where we all feel a lot of pain, whether we are Christians or whether we compromise. No matter who we are, we need to be able to be touched by the hurts of our friends. To be in the world is to be emotionally involved.

To be in the world is to be physically involved: to be in student government; involved in athletics (or the chess team); to be in the school choir, drama club, or cheerleading. If you have a 98.6 degree temperature, you ought to be involved in some extracurricular activities with your classmates.

To be in the world is to be mentally involved with your friends; to listen to them, to talk with them, to think about what they are thinking about, and to know how to logically communicate Jesus to them. After all, He is part of who you are.

To be in the world is to be socially involved in the world; to have friends spend the night at your house; to go to school football games, plays, and pep rallies; to go to a concert, the circus, or even just plain ol' McDonald's. To be socially involved in the world is healthy.

It is amazing how much we have in common with all people. We feel the same pain; we sit through the same classes; we wear basically the same clothes. We even pop the same type pimples.

We don't need diving bells. We don't even need snorkels, because we have the Lifeline to heaven living right inside us. He is the Holy Spirit, who isn't as concerned with the externals as He is with the internals. He is not as concerned with whom we hang around with as He is with how we behave when we are with them. This same Holy Spirit who produces holiness within us calls us to live holy lives in a very unholy society.

One way to be holy is to totally avoid any sinners (which is impossible), by locking yourself up in a sterilized diving bell. This is a man-made way that only causes worse problems. The other way is to learn to say, "No compromise." This, my friends, is God's way. And this is the only way to please Him.

To say "No compromise!" is to say "I know God made me just the way I am." It is to say, "Jesus has given me certain moral standards He wants me to keep so that I don't get hurt any more than is absolutely necessary." To say "No compromise!" is to say: "I don't have to lie about myself— or even exaggerate," "Here I am . . . take it or leave it!" "I love myself even though you might not understand." To say "No compromise!" is to say, "You want to make friends?" It is to say, "God, I trust you with my reputation," and to say, "I'd rather follow the Leader."

I wish I could leap off this page and throw my arms around you and tell you how much Jesus loves you. But Jesus did something more than leap off a page: He came down from heaven to show you His love. He felt your pain. He knows how tough it is to say, "No compromise!" After all, He says it all the time. And, He wants us to say it, because He knows it is the only way to really live.

Right now why don't you let Him throw His arms around you? I know those four words, *What will they think?* are crawling through your mind. But God is challenging you with four other words: *Dare to be different!*

Feelings

1. Have you ever gone to school feeling as if you were in a diving bell? Describe this sensation.
2. Why is it sometimes easier to avoid the world than to get into the world?
3. List some of the pains most students feel.
4. Why could this chapter be referred to as a nitroglycerin cocktail? How could it be misunderstood?

Thoughts

1. Why do people live in diving bells?
2. Define *worldliness*.
3. What specific areas of a worldly life-style were mentioned? What are some more?
4. What moral stand do most kids have trouble keeping? Why?
5. Why does Jesus tell His followers to get into the world?
6. Under what condition is it temporarily better not to get involved in the world?
7. What ways are Christians to get involved in the world?
8. Will you spend your life following Jesus, regardless of what others think?